# The Enlightened Manager

# The Enlightened Manager
## A Transformative Approach to Work and Life

Vishwanath Alluri
with
Harry Eyres

HARPER
BUSINESS

*An Imprint of* HarperCollins *Publishers*

First published in India by Harper Business 2025
An imprint of HarperCollins *Publishers*
HarperCollins *Publishers* India, Cyber City,
Building 10-A, Gurugram, Haryana - 122002, India
www.harpercollins.co.in

2 4 6 8 10 9 7 5 3 1

Copyright © Vishwanath Alluri 2025

P-ISBN: 978-93-6989-144-3
E-ISBN: 978-93-6989-076-7

The views and opinions expressed in this book are the author's own and the facts are as reported by him, and the publishers are not in any way liable for the same.

Vishwanath Alluri asserts the moral right
to be identified as the author of this work.

All rights reserved. No part of this publication may be reproduced, stored in a retrieval system, or transmitted, in any form or by any means, electronic, mechanical, photocopying, recording or otherwise, without the prior permission of the publishers.

Without limiting the exclusive rights of any author, contributor or the publisher of this publication, any unauthorized use of this publication to train generative artificial intelligence (AI) technologies is expressly prohibited. HarperCollins also exercise their rights under Article 4(3) of the Digital Single Market Directive 2019/790 and expressly reserve this publication from the text and data-mining exception.

Typeset in 11.5/15.1 Adobe Garamond Pro
by HarperCollins *Publishers* India Pvt. Ltd

Printed and bound at
Thomson Press (India) Ltd

This book is produced from independently certified FSC® paper
to ensure responsible forest management.

HarperCollins Publishers, Macken House, 39/40 Mayor Street Upper,
Dublin 1, D01 C9W8, Ireland

*This book is dedicated to all those who happen to read it with no expectations and preconceptions, and to those who happen to read it with expectations and preconceptions but are ready to examine their own expectations and preconceptions.*

# Contents

*Preface*   ix

1. The Why of the Book
   *In the spirit of bus-pushers*   1
2. Managing
   *The journey*   10
3. The Evolution
   *Explorers and colonizers*   18
4. Management Theories
   *Pundits and gurus*   24
5. Whole World of Jobs
   *First the whole and then the details*   31
6. Understanding Operations of the Mind
   *Core of management*   35
7. Result of Time
   *Time and conditioning*   52
8. Vulnerability
   *To be vulnerable is to live*   60

9. Brain and Computer
   *The analogy* — 65

10. Work-Life Balance
    *Coffee darshan, a pause in the day* — 71

11. The Unique Feel of Roger Federer
    *A golden era in tennis watching* — 104

12. Role Models
    *And second-hand human beings* — 120

13. Investors
    *Illusions, damned illusions and investor's dreams* — 131

14. Employees
    *Building blocks and shifting sands* — 139

15. Sales Management
    *Sense of wonderment* — 145

16. Finance Management
    *Finger on the pulse* — 154

17. Productivity
    *Three immutable laws* — 160

18. Beyond Business Schools
    *Nurturing the second horse* — 167

19. The Friend on the Bench
    *Awakening of intelligence* — 191

Epilogue
*Water in the hill* — 199

Notes — 203

# Preface

Language has influence on us, often more than we realize. Sometimes we are aware of this, but that is not always so. Language is used for communication—we make sounds and write words which are symbols of things. But we are so conditioned to mistake the word for the thing. I have been told, probably thousands of times, that the word is not the thing.

The word 'management' is a noun, according to English dictionaries. It might be better to think of it as a verb in the active present. It is not a fixed entity but a living process. A good manager is always busy and always free.

Similarly, I would like to clarify the meaning of the title of this book, in the hope of making its message as clear as possible.

The title is chosen rather consciously. I mean that I am conscious of the dangerous territory I am straying into, because in some esoteric quarters, the term 'enlightenment' denotes something transcendent and beyond description, almost beyond conception. This is not the meaning of the word I am intending here. However, in common parlance and according to the Collins English Dictionary, enlightened means: "Factually well-informed, tolerant of alternative opinions and guided by rational thought."

I have chosen the title 'The Enlightened Manager' according to the meaning given by the dictionary as I feel it communicates the burden of the book in a way that is relatable to most people.

The risk of keeping the title is purely mine. Taking risky initiatives and putting one's head onto a chopping block unwittingly goes naturally hand in hand with entrepreneurship.

"Coffee darshan" is another perhaps unfamiliar expression used in this book that needs some elaboration. In this context, I have to bring in a Spanish expression which seems to be somewhat related. "Sobremesa" is a beautiful tradition prevalent in Spain, and in Latin America, that doesn't have a direct translation in English but vaguely means a time to relax and savour the moment, often accompanied by coffee, tea, or a small liqueur. Coffee darshan is an expression coined by me and I don't think there is an equivalent expression in English. In any case, this is half English and half Indian. Darshan implies viewing wholesomely someone or something, mostly something admirable but, in this case, viewing one's own fallacies and sufferings. It is more profound than Sobremesa. Coffee darshan normally happens early morning or during the time of the day when you sip your favourite beverage, savouring that moment. But, more importantly, it provides an opportunity for a darshan, a viewing of one's own fallacies and mental sufferings. This moment is always fresh and exists only in the present, whether one is alone or in the company of friends. It has no accumulative quality. No doubt you might have enjoyed it in the past, but that moment was transitory; it has gone into the dead past. It exists only in the memory. Memory is always of the dead past.

During Sobremesa, people often share stories and they laugh, debate and connect deeply, sometimes for hours after the meal has ended. During coffee darshan, one goes beyond mere storytelling. Here people connect with each other in a relaxed setting and tend to share their inner problems with each other with an open heart. Here is a chance for darshan of one's own fallacies and of the fallacies and struggles of one's companion at the table. I am referring to mental states rather than physical sufferings. These possibilities exist whether one is sitting alone or in the company of friends. This viewing of one's own internal issues, living with one's own sufferings, is so vital in leading an orderly life. One normally escapes from suffering or suppresses suffering by rationalizing. But here, there is a different dimension altogether. How about staying with suffering and examining it instead of escaping or rationalizing. One has to test this out oneself and see what happens.

Another factor that gets in the way of a good coffee darshan at its own pace is the race of the life one is caught up in. Taking a moment off is viewed as an unproductive task and time wasted. It is so difficult to appreciate the value of a pause in the day.

In reality, this pause in the day has the potential to refresh you. You need to test this yourself. Maybe, this is the most productive moment of the day. In life, one goes through highs and lows daily. Who knows: it is possible that this pause in the day may offer you a clue as to how to go through pressure cooker situations with a touch of lightness.

Vishwanath Alluri

# 1

# The Why of the Book

## *In the spirit of bus-pushers*

---

Long ago, the village where my friend GP comes from was named Wet Hill, probably because there is damp ground to the north and hills—strangely shaped and red in colour—to the south. It is a place like many others in the interior of the southern part of the country—hot and dusty most of the year, though refreshed, at least in former times, by an ever-running river and shaded by trees. On the hill directly to the south of the village are two temples, one halfway up and one right on the top. They organize an annual festival, during which the villagers climb up the hill for refreshments in the two temples. Only some are capable of climbing to the top; others settle with having refreshments at the temple halfway up the hill. At the same time, many young people entertain themselves with gambling games next to the temple.

The village has no cafes and there isn't even a public telephone. There is a 'square' in the centre where people gather and where the spluttering old bus from the larger town arrives, stops and leaves, twice a day. Villagers, especially children, gather round to see who is arriving and who is leaving. As the bus is somewhat temperamental, it is a custom for the young and the older men to give the bus a push to get it started. They are known as the bus-pushers. They don't expect any reward for this.

They don't mind if their effort is not acknowledged by the bus driver or the bus conductor, who is also the ticket-giver. For them, pushing the bus until it starts is sort of a game. They don't regard it as a boring chore, done on compulsion or for reward. They just move away after the bus starts and don't even bother to look at the bus driver or any passenger in the bus to receive their compliments, if any.

On another day, long ago, the focus of attention in the village square was a very strange-looking person, with long, matted hair, a thick white beard, a huge turban, dirty clothes and a rather vacant expression. Some of those who got close to him also reported a rather strong odour.

This person was a 'godman'—that is to say, an object of veneration among certain villagers. The godman sat on the bench, staring into space. Occasionally, he would make gestures, nod or shake his head. Very rarely did he speak.

At the godman's feet was a tin container for food—a tiffin—brought to him by his 'worshippers'. Although it was hard to make sense of either his gestures or his utterances, there were several people in the assembled company who claimed to understand them—and indeed asserted they were of great significance. One may wonder what a godman has to do with management. You will find reference to this in later chapters of this book. It is to this kind of godmen many gullible minds fall prey, and corporate managers are no exception.

My friend GP likes to tell the story of a different sort of a man, a farmer from the same village known as Panna. GP grew up close to Panna and is well acquainted with his ways. He is an important character in this book. Panna was known throughout the region, for his fields were always lush with grain.

'Have you ever done anything spontaneously without being asked to do and without expecting anything in return?'

– *Friend on the Bench*[1]

One day, a neighbouring villager said to his son, 'Go learn from him: how does the earth yield so much for him.' So the young boy travelled all the way by bus to Panna's and asked, 'Can you teach me how to be a good farmer like you?'

Panna replied, 'I can't teach you. Good farming cannot be taught. But it can be learnt if you have an open mind. You need to work at least two crops with me.'

That was a surprise to the young man, who thought he could learn everything in one week and go away.

'If you just want to learn in one week or one month,' replied Panna, 'there's a big building over there. That's the agricultural college. You can get certificates from there. But the core aspects can't be taught. They can be learnt. Come and stay with me.'

So the young man went to stay with Panna. They made an arrangement about boarding and lodging. But the young man was surprised to learn that Panna slept in the cattle shed with the cattle. 'We need to mind them to take care of them,' said Panna. 'In the morning, we take out the manure, we take the cattle out, feed them, bathe them. It's not just about doing things according to a regular schedule; when the cattle look at me in a certain way, I can sense their needs—all from the look in their eyes. So we are feeding them, taking care of them, we are cleaning the cattle shed. All that gives you a feeling of the health of the beast. We have a direct relationship with the cattle. We could call that "the feel." So when you take them to the farm to work, their response will be different.

We can test it out. You are not a stranger to them. You take care of their livelihood.'

On the second day, Panna asked the young man, 'Why do you want to go into farming?'

The young man replied, 'I want to have a good life, I want to have a good crop, I want to win awards, make money, lead a comfortable life.'

Panna replied, 'Farming is not a means of living, but a way of living. We're dealing with passion. Farming is about more than making a living—it's about living and making a connection to the land. That is farming. How one takes care of the land. Relationship to the land, to the earth, and to people, and to animals—that's the heart of it. Farmers produce food and fibre, not products; products come from factories. Food and fibre come from the land. No machine, no piece of technology can replace the eye of the farmer, in caring for animals or crops or appreciating the land.'

Let me tell you about this book. It is based on conversations I, the writer, also known as HC, have been having with my friend GP, a tech entrepreneur, who founded a transnational tech company which was acquired by a tech giant from the US. For most of the time, GP had Panna as his companion to exchange his thoughts and feelings with—more as a sounding board and not as a guru.

Ultimately, the decisions GP made were his own and not borrowed from Panna. In fact, Panna would insist upon that basic premise, that he should not be taken as a preacher or a pundit. According to him, it should all come down to GP's own perception: that should be the guiding light. Panna, in turn, had been deeply struck by what his Friend on the Bench had said in many different contexts, and in many different ways, about the various complex issues of life and human relationships.

According to Panna, this Friend on the Bench is the rarest of rare occurrences in the world. This friend went around the world talking and discussing with human beings what they experienced as problems of living. This he did for nearly sixty years, not as a guru or a preacher but more as a friend sitting on a bench in the park. Hence, in this book, he is referred to as the Friend on the Bench.

Apparently, Masayoshi Son, founder of SoftBank Group, a big name in the world of investment, suffered massive losses due to his investment in WeWork, an office space-sharing company based in New York. In one of his press conferences, Son said that he wished that he had had the benefit of the company of Yoda, a fictional character in *Star Wars*. Yoda, by the way, is a Jedi Master who is small in stature but revered for his wisdom.

We might speculate that it would have been better if Masayoshi Son had known about the Friend on the Bench, who was a real human being, instead of referring to a fictional character such as Yoda of *Star Wars*. As Panna explained to GP, the Friend on the Bench never acted like a guru or preached anything, but always talked with the freshness of a breeze and investigated the problems hand in hand with his interlocutor. It is up to the interlocutor how to see and act on the truth of the matter, using their own intelligence. So what the Friend on the Bench is trying to do is awaken your intelligence by posing the right questions and letting you enquire into them and discover the truth of the matter for yourself.

You could say the book gives a farmer-like perspective on management. Before we say why this book is written, we need to say something about two tools that have great value in life. One is the tool of negation—finding out what something is not before deciding what it is—and the other is the mirror of relationship. We cannot see ourselves directly; we can only do so in the mirror of relationship. Both of these are at the core of management.

It is also worth saying that we have not written this book in order to achieve fame and glory for ourselves. As with tennis, as with so many things, getting caught up in the outcome is going to spoil the very process of writing this book. Our work is more like that of the bus-pushers.

So let us start with the following premise. In any company, the relationship with people is fundamental.

If you have 30-40 people in a company, the manager can watch them when they come in at 9 or 9.30 in the morning, how reluctantly, how enthusiastically. See how they sit at their desk—how many of them are really enthusiastic. Some people sit with their heads in their hands. Then there's a problem—the CEO of a small company can see that. The CEO can talk to that person, talk to them nicely, ask what's wrong. He knows, for instance, that this guy got married six months earlier. That implies some natural consequences—perhaps, there is an uneasy relationship between the mother and the wife. This is not unknown in India, and maybe other parts of the world. So the CEO talks to him—it's part of caring, taking care.

Another subject farmers talk about is sowing the seed. When the sowing season starts, you must sow the seeds. The good farmer can feel the quality of the seeds at the time of buying them in the market. At the time he buys the seeds, he can feel the potency of the seed by touching it. He doesn't want to waste his time; if you plant poor quality seeds, you wait for six months and then nothing of great value happens. It's a waste of time. That applies to management also. When you take some new initiatives, recruiting new people, you must have a feel for the people and the project.

So the story we told was about this farmer, Panna. The story is also about the professors. The professors are there, speaking a lot of words; you can take lessons from them, but they are not getting their hands dirty. The farmer is not teaching the young man anything, but he's making him learn. A professor is about things, a farmer is the thing. A professor talks about farming whereas a farmer talks of farming, and farmer's talk is made with a feel of the reality. We mean a talk by someone who has only theoretical knowledge of farming and a talk by someone who has direct hands on the feel of farming.

In the pages that follow, we will ask what can and cannot be taught about management. We will go beyond business schools, we hope, but not by being more ambitious, rather by being more modest. We use the tool of negation—first of all establishing what management is not—before coming to some understanding of what the core of it might be. We will also delve into relationships as management is about managing people, not about doing the work yourself. But at a deeper level, it is about the state of the mind. So I must understand my state of mind first. In management, the real soil is the state of mind. You must care for your state of mind first. Let's say you're provoked by somebody, somebody upsetting you, or you feel jealous or angry: the seed of anger takes root in the soil of the mind. Our book is about understanding the operation of the mind using the tool of negation and the mirror of relationship. In the same way, for the farmer, the soil is a way of living, not a means of living. The soil is the state of mind.

We bring in a number of other topics.

There will be chapters on topics such as investors, role models, sales management, finance management, employees, and productivity. And in a separate chapter, we discuss the unique 'feel' of Roger Federer.

So it is in this spirit of feeling things directly—as with Panna and the young man—that this book is written. The first-hand spirit. How this can be approached by someone with this farmer-like approach to management.

To understand this approach, let us take the example of tennis. Since it is a technical game, one needs a coach to teach all the techniques—you hold the racket a particular way, you hit the ball in a manner. But having an eye for a ball, that, GP says, can't be taught, even though the coach can tell his student to keep her eye on the ball. This—keeping one's eye on the ball—only happens in the moment. This is a dynamic process, not an accumulative experience. The player may have been a Grand Slam winner some ten years back. But this won't help him when he goes out on court on day one of the eleventh year. He has to remain fresh and this keeping eye on the ball is the first-hand spirit we like to expound in this book.

People speak about 'anger management', and indeed many attend anger management courses. But so long as we regard our anger as separate from ourselves, we will not go far. Here we are discussing something else—being aware of your anger in the moment. So perhaps you don't tell your employee he's bungled it. Maybe it's possible for you to go beyond the state of anger. Maybe it's not possible. But, at least at the end of the day, you can replay that like a slow-motion replay on TV. This is important for managers; even if you can't do it in the moment, at the end of the day, or some time, somewhere, you can revisit it. Slow motion enables you to see everything, how the ball is moving, whether you're in the right position to receive it. That may do something good for you, bring some order. In the end, the emphasis is seeing in the moment and not in retrospect.

In tennis, when you're hitting the ball, you need to watch the ball, not the target. If you're watching the target you're going to mess it up. Most managers and entrepreneurs are caught up with the end target, most of the time. Startups are very much inspired by big success stories, high valuation. Most of them are all the time caught up in outcome. They don't pay attention to what is at hand. In sport, some people mistake the scoreboard for the game. The best players see through all that and take the ball on its merit.

Eyesight cannot be substituted. Nobody can teach you this. You have to see it yourself. And sometimes you can have the benefit of a replay.

# 2

# Managing

## *The Journey*

---

You know how it is on long flights, especially at night? You sleep fitfully, if at all, and your mind wanders, in and out of clarity and consciousness. I am both excited and apprehensive. It's been so long since I was in the country of my birth. My parents were British agronomists who worked in southern India. I was educated there in my early years, before I came back to Britain.

I'm looking forward to seeing my friend GP, to visiting his home city, which I don't know at all, before we set off on our road trip down to the village. His village, and mine also, though I left it when I was a small child and remember very little about it. He still has family and other connections there, visits from time to time, and is involved in a certain project he's going to show me.

Our road trip is also going to be a series of conversations around a theme, I gather. I'm a writer by profession and GP is an entrepreneur, who nowadays devotes much of his time to the work of the institutions left behind by the Friend on the Bench. GP's idea is for us to discuss management and entrepreneurship—not as they're normally discussed or taught in schools, but going back to first principles, as it were. I'm a little nervous about this as I'm no expert on management or entrepreneurship; I've spent my life in solitary pursuits, studying and writing.

Returning to the village is not a random choice. That's where GP received his formative influences from the farmer, Panna. Panna in turn learned from a more mysterious figure, the Friend on the Bench, a master of reality. This man had travelled the world talking to human beings for over sixty years, not as a guru or a philosopher but as a friend sitting on a bench.

I never knew the Friend on the Bench, but I was exposed to some of his talks and discussions with a cross spectrum of people—laymen to scholars—when I attended the school he founded not far from our village. Exposure to his talks and the interactions he had with various people has enabled GP and me to gain some degree of clarity in life; nowadays, it is what we mainly talk about when we meet. When GP thinks about management, he tells me, his mind turns first not to any management guru but to the Friend on the Bench, the master of reality.

I eventually fall asleep, and wake up as we are coming in to land. My first feeling is that this is not the country I remember. The international airport could be the airport of any large city anywhere. As I proceed, rather bleary-eyed, through immigration and then to collect my baggage from the revolving belt, I feel a certain sense of dislocation. Perhaps the smell is slightly different; yes, there are women in saris as well as men in business suits. But this is not the land of my childhood or the land I have imagined.

It's still dark outside, though dawn is breaking, and the dawn chorus has begun. That at least hasn't changed. I call my friend GP to tell him I've arrived; he's arranged a taxi to take me to the hotel. The taxi driver is a lean, eager young man who tells me the journey will take about an hour.

The light comes in quickly and it's already warm. We drive through straggly outskirts of what seems a vast metropolis. Great tower blocks have arisen or are under construction as far as the eye can see. Everything looks dusty and parched. It's the dry season; several months still to go before the monsoon starts. We enter a raised freeway—'it's 17 kilometres long', my driver proudly informs me. After a few kilometres we pass an office building shaped like a fish—'the Fish Building', comments my driver. A fish out of water perhaps. The buildings are getting more dense and I guess we are nearing the heart of the city, but in truth there are few landmarks.

Maybe it's my state after the long flight and dislocation, but I feel I cannot make sense of all this—it's too vast, too sprawling. I expect the feeling will change.

We arrive at the hotel—an imposing modern building with a vast open atrium, filled with medium-sized trees. There is a guarded gateway. I pass through security; my bags are X-rayed separately. Once again I feel I could be anywhere. But I am glad and grateful to find my comfortable room and take a shower, then a short rest.

When I go down, GP is there to meet me in the lobby and take me out to a traditional dosa breakfast. The restaurant he chooses was started in 1950s by a passionate restauranteur hailing from a place in Karnataka, a neighbouring state, well known for its vegetarian cuisine, especially dosas. It could hardly be more different from the sleek modern hotel: it looks as if it hasn't been refurbished since the 1950s, everything different shades of beige and brown, utilitarian-looking but to me full of character. Now I know I'm in India. The dosa served with local coffee is delicious.

GP looks just the same as when I last saw him a couple of years ago—white shirt, dark trousers, well-trimmed dark hair with just a hint of grey. He's never been in the least ostentatious in his manner and appearance. Lowkey you could say, but he radiates energy and his manner is warm.

We catch up a little bit on what's been happening in our lives—my latest book, his travels—and then I start asking questions.

'So tell me more about this trip, GP. Where are we going? What's the purpose of it? What are we going to discuss on the way?'

GP chuckles. 'That sounds a bit like life, doesn't it? But with life we don't know the ending. With this trip we are going back to the village.'

'Ah yes, the village. I wonder whether I'll remember anything about it.'

'Well, some things have changed but others haven't. The bus, the bus-pushers, the bench, the tree. Maybe some of the crops have changed. Not so many people keep their animals in the house. The village school. But I'm working on a water project there. I'll show you.'

'Of course, Panna, your friend, the farmer you told me so much about, is no longer there.'

'No, Panna died quite a few years back. He is still remembered in the village.'

'And the Friend on the Bench?'

'You know his story as well as I do. His life ended far from here, in another country, but the school he founded, which you attended, and which is not far from the village, still flourishes. You should know he talked of whole of life. Education of children is an important part of his teachings. But I am not sure you can put him in the category of educators, as the world has known them. He is an educator of life itself. Though he has passed away, I think the truth of what he talked about is always alive as long as you are serious about life.'

I thought for a moment of that man who I never met, but whose voice and face I knew so well. The many talks I have listened to, given at schools and gatherings all over the world, his gentle but persisting questioning, asking always the most pertinent questions, never avoiding anything.

'It'll take us some time to get there, I suppose.'

'Yes, we'll stop at a couple of places on the way. We'll travel at ease. And we have things to discuss.'

'Ah yes, the book we're writing. Something to do with management and entrepreneurship, from an unusual angle.'

'Yes, we'll go into that this evening. First I want to show you something of my city.'

GP's home city feels like more than one city. We head first to the centre and reach the large placid expanse of the great lake which separates the old city from the new city. Around here are remnants of the British Raj, clubs and grand Victorian buildings. The lake isn't pristine, but at least the water gives a sense of freshness and coolness amid the heat and the dust. Behind the large sized statue of Buddha, I can see the great towers and office blocks of the gleaming new metropolis, the city of tech. All this has sprung up in the last ten or fifteen years.

Quite the opposite sense comes from the great four-turreted gateway at the heart of the old southern part of the city. This is teeming, bustling India, a great mass of people, rickshaws, bazaars—a whole street of them selling just bangles; another street of jewelers specializing in pearls; another of saris. 'Saris are still very important in India, HC. Sales never drop in that line of business.'

'Sounds like what they say about champagne, GP—in defeat you need it, in victory you deserve it.'

After a while we head away from the Gate and surrounding bazaars. GP has one more site to show me before we return to my hotel for an early evening meal.

I had heard vaguely of the tombs as one of the lesser known wonders of India but nothing prepares me for their beauty and grace. Their enclosure is a few kilometres outside the city, close to a vast ancient fort, really a fortified city. For years now the tombs, dating back to the sixteenth and seventeenth centuries, have been undergoing a thorough restoration. The work is carrying on because there are no fewer than eighty-two tombs, all with graceful domes and intricate decoration which blends Persian and Indian influences.

These are the tombs of the rulers, their wives and others—dancers and singers (who were consorts of the rulers), doctors—who gained an equality of respect in death. They are spaced apart, with ample surrounds and basins of water, and many mature trees. The atmosphere of peace is in startling contrast to so much else in this city, in India, in the world.

Somehow, we find we have acquired a guide. We didn't exactly hire him, it was more that he attached himself to us. He has a well-practised patter but we're not sure that we trust all the information he gives us. There's one phrase he keeps using—'makes sense?'—even when what he's just said makes no sense at all.

Now, finally, as the day draws to a close, I feel I am in India, with all its extremes of beauty and ugliness, of immense wealth and desperate poverty, with something that never seems to change. As we make our way back to the hotel, I am both tired and excited.

Over dinner—GP has suggested a traditional biryani with side-dishes—we finally get down to 'business'.

'Our trip seems quite symbolic,' I suggest. 'As if you, or you and I, are retracing our steps, going back to the beginning. To where we both started, before we set out on our different journeys, in my case my writing journey and in yours your tech-entrepreneurial journey. At least that's what I assume you did. I have to admit I have little idea what "being an entrepreneur" really means.'

'I told you the value of "the feel" in whatever one is doing something instinctively, something very hands on, in the way a farmer has a feel for the health and state of his animals, quality of seeds, the workers on the farm, caring for the earth.

'Panna said my entrepreneurial journey was based more on technical ignorance and business innocence. I agreed, but the key thing was that I knew I was ignorant, technically speaking.

'Also, I can't claim to be innocent in a childlike way. The innocence of a child is altogether different. Business innocence for me meant not expecting anything in return like a trader at the end of each day's work.'

## Be aware but not be caught in it

'You didn't study business or management, did you? I remember you trained as an accountant.'

'Correct. I studied accountancy, which I still consider a very useful basis. At a certain point, I was considering different paths. Members of my family, as you know, were quite politically engaged. There was a strong motivation to improve the lives of poor people who had so little. But I got to know a few prominent politicians, one of whom went on to become President of the country and another Prime Minister and I decided that was not going to be my path.'

'And then you worked for various companies and eventually decided you would set up your own tech business. How has it worked out?'

'All I would say is that it is not about success but it is about non-failure. We have not failed to return to investors what they invested in the company. This is not about me, but there were certain things, in my view, one would not want to do. For example, to be a labour contractor. Or to be part of the mortgaging of India. It is also the reluctance to work under stupid bosses that paved the path to entrepreneurship.'

'So what will we be addressing in this little book of ours, GP? Will we be giving people advice on how to be managers or entrepreneurs?'

'Let us forget giving advice. Who are we to give advice? Why should anyone take our advice? I am not sure management can be taught. But we can enquire into it, using the tool of negation and the tool of mirror of relationship, as articulated by the Friend on the Bench. First of all, perhaps, and starting tomorrow, when we go to visit the Business School, we can find out something about the prevailing theories of management, who the current management gurus are, and what they have to offer.'

It is getting late, and I am tired after the journey. GP and I agree to meet next morning at his favourite café.

I wake up refreshed after a long sleep. When I open the blinds, I take in the view from my hotel bedroom window, beyond a busy commercial street, a large green space—perhaps a park. I am relieved this city still has parks and greenery. GP has told me that today we will be visiting one of the country's most prestigious business schools, in its own campus just outside the city centre. We will be meeting a few professors and students informally. We want to get an idea of what they think management is about.

GP has chosen one of his favourite cafes. 'Café Being' has tables out in front and a terrace at the back looking over a small but beautiful park. There's a fresh warm smell of roasted coffee beans as I walk in and a tempting array of cakes.

GP launches in without any preliminaries. 'I want to talk about what they teach at management schools and whether that helps you become a manager. And more fundamentally whether management can actually be taught.'

'There certainly seems to be no shortage of management schools in the world. Are you saying they're selling snake oil? But first answer me a simple question: Is a manager different from an entrepreneur? I'm confused about this.'

# 3

# The Evolution

*Explorers and colonizers*

---

'Entrepreneur sounds like a contemporary term and I suppose here we are thinking especially about what are known as tech entrepreneurs. But the history of entrepreneurship goes back to much earlier times. What were men like Christopher Columbus and Captain Cook if not entrepreneurs?'

'They were explorers, no?'

'They were going into uncharted waters, taking great risks, risking their lives in fact. Cook lost his life when he was clubbed to death while attempting to kidnap the king of Hawaii. But they were not just explorers, they were also in a sense colonizers. Columbus paved the way for the Spanish kings and conquistadors to dominate the Americas. Cook claimed Australia for the English crown.'

'Are you saying some tech companies nowadays are like colonizers?'

'Today's new tech ventures "boldly go" into unknown areas and dominate their particular domain when they succeed. This domination can be equated with colonizing. Compare the ways in which Microsoft, Google, even Facebook for that matter have become so dominant in their domains.

## Industrialists: Capital intensive

'In the 19th century, entrepreneurs—we call them industrialists—developed heavy industries such as steel making, railways, ship-building and so on. These were capital-intensive industries that required heavy injections of capital and much plant.

'After this period of heavy industry came the growth of services sectors like travel, insurance, and banking.'

## Knowledge workers: Alvin Toffler's Third Wave

'Then came what the writer on the evolution of technology Alvin Toffler has called the Third Wave. This essentially meant development of technologies which were knowledge-based or entirely founded on intellectual work. Here the capital investment was not a vital ingredient for starting up a company. Anyone with a bright technology idea could take the plunge. And this is what inspires or motivates so many young people today.'

'But very few succeed?'

'There is clearly something else needed, beyond having a bright idea. On quite another level are the underlying passion and love of doing the work in the chosen area. This is not something quick and simple to grasp—or to teach. Time and time again it has been proved that it is not the mere technology idea that takes the venture far, but rather that the key ingredient is the love of doing or passion of the entrepreneur.'

'I get you. That was what Panna said to the young man who wanted to be a "successful" farmer. That he could go to agricultural college and learn all sorts of techniques but that would not make him a farmer. Do you mean to say that one cannot become a manager by simply attending a business school?'

'It looks like that. You know that Steve Jobs and Bill Gates, two of the most successful businessmen in history, didn't attend any business school.'

'Yes I did know that.'

## Two Classes of Businesses

'And while we're about this, we should also distinguish two classes of businesses. It is about the relationship between technologies and businesses. One class consists of technology development companies, which you could also call technology businesses; the other consists of old businesses adopting new technologies.'

'Give me examples.'

'For instance, Amazon is a typical old-style business using new technologies that created a new way of buying goods, books and so on. Similarly, booking.com has brought booking hotel accommodation onto a new technology platform. Microsoft, Oracle are technology development businesses. Besides these there are also totally new businesses using new technologies—something at a completely different level. A company like Google is a new technology business, a unique blend of new technology and a new business. Similarly Apple has pioneered many original new products—iPod, iPhone, iPad.'

GP pauses and we both take a sip of Café Being's delicious coffee. None of this is familiar ground to me, but I can tell GP is passionate about it.

'Forgive me if I'm lecturing here,' says GP.

'Don't worry, I'm learning.'

## B2B and B2C

'So to continue: there's another way of looking at the current technology scene from a management perspective—one can divide ventures into ones that operate on the "business-to-business" model and those that operate on a "business-to-consumer" model.'

'We're talking about where the primary interface is?'

'Yes that's right. I'll try to explain. PayPal, for instance, is a business-to-consumer operation. Companies such as Oracle and IBM work on a business-to-business model. So also do many tech companies involved in developing data infrastructure who sell their technologies to big enterprises. Cisco—a data infrastructure company which is at the core of the internet world—is an excellent example of the business-to-business model, though a typical householder also may buy its Wi-Fi routers for their domestic use.

## Qualities of a farmer and of a trader

'It's extremely useful to keep this distinction in mind when one is pitching to start a new venture, or even just thinking about doing so. The business-to-business model has much in common with the way of working of a farmer, whereas the business-to-consumer model takes you into the domain of a merchant.'

'Could you explain that? I'm not sure I understand.'

'The qualities of a farmer and a merchant are very different. Also their motivations. A farmer committed in his heart does what he or she does out of love and concern. It is not just a job, but a passion. Such a farmer looks towards the long-term health of his crops or animals. But a merchant is mainly interested in selling and marketing. This can be quite short-term; advertising and persuading the consumer are the name of the game. The art of persuasive imagery—advertising—comes into play.

'This distinction between the qualities of a farmer and the qualities of a merchant is crucial when you are looking at the difference between business-to-business and business-to-consumer domains. If you are an entrepreneur, this distinction is valuable when you are starting a new venture. An entrepreneur who has more of the qualities of a farmer will probably be suited to the business-to-business segment whereas an entrepreneur with the characteristics and skills of a merchant will have more to offer working in the business-to-consumer segment.'

So it's essential to know your own qualities. And maybe many are not clear on this.

## Manager and Entrepreneur

'But one thing I'm wondering about is this: is the entrepreneur separate from the manager? How do we distinguish these terms?'

'As I see it, HC, an entrepreneur, also often called a founder, is not separate from a manager. In fact, entrepreneurship is part of management. Or you could say they are intertwined. There are managers who are entrepreneurial, and it is no hindrance for a manager to be entrepreneurial. In fact, if a manager can relate to the state of mind of the entrepreneur, he could be like a cofounder of the venture.'

'So it appears once again that it is the understanding of one's state of the mind, that is at the heart of understanding what one is.'

'An entrepreneur can be compared to a farmer who also has to work on the farm along with the workers. The key distinction between the two is that the fundamental decisions like, for instance which crop to grow on the farm, or which livestock to choose, is made by the farmer. Similarly an entrepreneur makes the decision about the nature of his or her startup business and of the product he or she is aiming to develop.'

'Does the entrepreneur do this entirely on his or her own?'

'In the process of his decision making about the choice of the crop, the farmer could also involve other workers. Similarly an entrepreneur could also bounce his or her ideas about a new venture with her connections. Once the decision is made about this, the farmer also is another worker on the farm like any other worker though he may have the authority to oversee the work on the farm. An entrepreneur also has to work like any other manager once the new venture starts though he has the overall responsibility of managing the venture. So we can say once the venture starts to get going the entrepreneur is the manager.'

'And is this what they teach in the management schools?'

'I don't know. But we'll see. Time to set off for the school.'

We leave Café Being—with some regret on my part—and walk down a leafy lane to the main road, where we find the car which will take us to the business school. Our route takes us through part of the city and then out west, where the new hi-tech area is located. Before we reach the business school and meet with students and professors I want to ask GP about management books and prevailing theories of management.

# 4

# Management Theories
## *Pundits and gurus*

---

'I'm blissfully ignorant about management theory, GP. But I know you've made something of a study of it. Who in your view are the management thinkers or great gurus?'

'Firstly I must confess I am not a scholar. But based on whatever is known to me, I think we should start with the great Austrian economist Joseph Schumpeter.'

'Didn't he say something about capitalism being "creative destruction"? Sounds a bit like what the Silicon Valley crowd are saying now—disruptive technologies.'

'Yes—though he actually borrowed that phrase from Werner Sombart—but with differences. He was perhaps a little more favourably inclined towards democracy than some of the Silicon Valley characters. Schumpeter was probably the first person to theorize extensively about entrepreneurship.'

'He was pro-entrepreneur?'

'Yes. In fact he attributed most of the innovation—"the doing of old things in a new way or new things in a new way"—in society to entrepreneurs or what he called 'wild spirits.'

'And who comes after Schumpeter?'

'I would single out three or four. Peter Drucker claimed to establish management "as a discipline in its own right". He held that management is "not business management but the governing organ of all institutions in modern society". Drucker talked about managing yourself.'

'And he had a point?'

'Yes, but I would say he didn't go far enough, or deep enough: he didn't get to what I see as the core of management.'

'How do you mean?'

'His idea of managing yourself was external; he spoke in terms of one's strengths and weaknesses, values, "performance", "feedback analysis", "remedying bad habits" and so on. He never went into what managing yourself could actually mean. Others of the so-called great gurus had feet of clay. And by the way Drucker had a rather a good comment on management gurus: 'I have been saying for many years that we are only using the word "guru" because "charlatan" is too long to fit into a headline.' It appears that this concept of values is at the root of business education which despite professing to "make the world a better place" is maybe failing in that aim. We will talk about this when we touch on the education provided in business schools.'

'So who are these other so-called gurus?'

'Tom Peters, not a guru, but someone who came to be perceived as a guru because he wrote a well-received book *In Search of Excellence*. It became a bestseller. A series of television programmes based on the book appeared on PBS in America, with Peters hosting. The primary idea involved solving business problems with as few business-process overheads as possible. Later it came in for a lot of criticism. Merrill R. (Rick) Chapman, the managing editor of *Softletter*, an online newsletter covering the business of software marketing, wrote a book on high-tech marketing fiascos which he called *In Search of Stupidity*. Chapman noted that 'with only a few exceptions [the excellent companies were] large firms with dominant positions in markets that were senescent or static.'

Suddenly, a voice comes from the dashboard of the car. In fact it seems to be emanating from the figure of the farmer seated on a bench with an empty space next to him, under the rear view mirror. The voice is that of an older man, friendly, experienced. He has the accent of our native village. He appears to have been listening to our conversation. 'In fact Tom Peters went on to become a highly paid speaker in the speaker circuit, did he not, GP, unlike you who are so conditioned in your role as CEO that you speak mainly to a paid audience.'

We are both startled. GP chuckles. It dawns on me: this is Panna speaking.

'Is this some new-fangled piece of tech, GP?'

GP puts his finger to his lips. As Panna seems to go quiet, I carry on.

'What you're talking about certainly doesn't sound like an exact science.'

'No, not really. In essence what Tom Peters has done to claim his fame was to write a book on management after interviewing hundreds of managers of so-called successful companies. But later he admitted to faking some of the data. So for any youngster to follow what is written in the book and start his managerial journey might be an immense delusion.'

Once again there resonates the voice from the car dashboard. 'To me it sounds like journeying from second hand to third hand. But why don't you have a look at the business school and then we can talk about it further.'

## Management Schools—Branding and Networking

We are at the gates of a beautiful-looking campus.

There's a long, curving drive through immaculately maintained lawns leading to an impressive set of buildings faced with marble. A circular drum-like building is approached via an immense hallway.

We are greeted by two professors and led into the building and up to a seminar room where we are to meet students. We are told of the success this school has achieved in international rankings—among the top ten such schools in the world—and of the notable positions held by alumni. Truly this seems like a gateway to fortune.

The students are a well-mannered, bright-looking bunch. They are studying Finance, Public Policy, Entrepreneurship. They respond to questions intelligently. I'm impressed. They seem to have a grasp of the basics. One speaks of 'the intersection of strategy and leadership.' Another says a 'manager gets things done.' Another mentions an exercise in team dynamics she has found useful. 'It was about how to get people, who are very different in character and approach, to work towards a common goal.' But I can tell GP isn't entirely satisfied.

Driving back from the immaculate campus, GP looks thoughtful. He finally comes out with the question: 'Can management actually be taught?'

'Apparently yes,' I reply. 'Look at all these excellent well-prepared students. At the range of courses they are studying. And because this is a highly ranked school, no doubt many or most of them will find the positions they are looking for.'

I can tell GP is not convinced.

'So you were impressed by all that, were you? The grandeur of the buildings and so on.' Panna is speaking from the car dashboard. 'I'd say that buildings don't make a school. What makes a school is the network of relationship that exists among all the players in the game, that is the professors, students, administrators, directors on the board of management, staff working there. And that in turn has to do with the state of mind of all these stakeholders. Think of the professors—some are contractual, looking for a job security in promotion, switching to an American university, joining a global corporation or trying to gain tenure. Students are on the look-out for lucrative connections. Unless they are all on the same page at the same time what we have is mere buildings which are cement and concrete structures. If they have great architecture, maybe the architect can showcase his work to another potential client. If the interior is beautiful the interior designer can use this place as his showroom.'

There is a pause. Then GP asks, 'What do we mean by teaching, by education? Is it just about acquiring some letters, BA, MA, MBA which are a passport to a job?'

## Technique Vs Moment of Life

'If you're asking me, GP,' booms the voice from the car dashboard, 'we want to experience life as a whole, that's what we mean by education, and a set of techniques can't give us the capacity to do that. Speaking as a farmer I think one can learn by direct experience, by putting one's hands to the earth. Nowadays it's quite different. Young people are filled with techniques and theories. But that turns them into mere instruments, into specialists. They may gain knowledge about their specialism but they cannot experience life as a whole.'

I decide to ask Panna a question. 'Surely there's a place for techniques in this complicated modern world of ours.'

'There is a place for techniques,' replies Panna. 'But techniques should not dominate. Too much emphasis on techniques distorts everything. Above all, we should not teach children that technique is all that matters. They must become human beings, not technicians. But I've already said enough.'

Panna's voice is fading away and it falls silent. GP and I look at one another for a moment.

## Validity of what is said and not who said it

'I know what you're thinking but don't question it,' offers GP. 'I think the important thing is this: we should just look at the validity of what is said. It is not about who said it; it is more about what is said.'

'And how does that relate to business schools, and what we've just seen?'

'Just the other day I read a couple of articles about business schools. One, in the *Financial Times*, was a review of a book by Martin Parker titled "Shut Down the Business Schools: What's Wrong with Management Education". The other, co-written by the well-known writers Warren Bennis and James O'Toole, published in the *Harvard Business Review*, was also extremely scathing about business schools. They argued, in essence, that most of the people teaching in business schools had never run a business, and probably wouldn't know how to. 'We cannot imagine a professor of surgery who has never seen a patient,' they said, 'or a piano teacher who doesn't play the instrument, and yet today's business schools are packed with intelligent, highly trained faculty with little or no managerial experience… business education in this country is devoted overwhelmingly to technical training…[but] executives who fail—financially as well as morally—rarely do so from a lack of expertise. Rather, they fail because they lack interpersonal skills and practical wisdom.' And this view was echoed by Ray Kroc, the CEO of McDonalds and inspiration of Mark Knopfler's brilliant song Boom Like That. Kroc had no time at all for business school graduates. He thought they lacked drive and market savvy. For a long time McDonalds had a policy of not hiring business school graduates. But we will go into all this further another time.'

We make our way back to the city mostly in silence, each pursuing his own thoughts. We arrange to have supper at GP's house.

GP's house, when I get here around nightfall, is in a quiet green area of the city. I ring the bell and am greeted by GP. Everything is immaculately clean and tidy and there is an absence of clutter. Inwardly, I sigh as I reflect on the piles of books and papers in my study at home.

GP's wife, who is out for the evening, has prepared a delicious vegetarian meal, and we catch up on family stories.

Then we return to work.

# 5

# Whole World of Jobs

*First the whole and then the details*

---

'If you look at what people do for a living,' begins GP, 'there is a wide spectrum of jobs or means of livelihood. Some are much easier—for an outsider—to understand than others. We might struggle to comprehend what is involved in the work of a rocket scientist; when it comes to a barber, it is somewhat simpler to grasp what the job entails. But is there a way of understanding the nature of all jobs?'

'That seems a Herculean task.'

'When the problem is complex, the approach needs to be simple. We should get a grasp of the whole first and then the details. Is there a simple way to understand what is involved in all the jobs that one can conceivably do in the world?

'Here is an approach—a way of cutting the Gordian knot, if you like. The right approach seems to be understanding the state of mind of the person involved. What if you divide all the jobs that exist into two categories, technical and non-technical?'

'Well, that seems relatively uncontroversial, though I'm not quite sure what you mean.'

'By a technical job we mean all those jobs where one works with a machine or mechanically or with a technical device. For instance, what a software programmer does is regarded as technical. His work relies on knowledge and experience in a programming language like Java or whatever programming language or tools he is using; he uses it to write software code on a computer. The knowledge he uses is stored in the brain or in a book.

'Similarly, a pilot is using his knowledge and experience in doing the work of piloting an aeroplane. Even a barista in a coffee shop is doing a technical job.'

'I'm not sure about that. I have many interactions with baristas and the human touch is extremely important.'

'You are probably right. At least we can say a nontechnical job involves dealing with other human beings rather than with machines and technical devices. The job of a manager, for that matter an administrator in a nonprofit, is essentially non-technical as his or her work at all times involves dealing with other human beings. I like what Harold Koontz, a writer on management has said: "Management is an art of getting things done through and with the people in formally organized groups."'

## More of 'How' and less of 'What'

'A manager', continues GP, 'may have a high-level understanding of what is involved in the technical work the team is engaged in but he himself or she herself is not involved in doing the work which is assigned to the team member. We can say while the team member is involved in "what" of it, the manager is involved in the "how" of it. This is because his job most of the time consists of overseeing the work of the team member. Management is not the "what" of it; rather it is "how" of it.'

'So you are saying good management is not just what is backstage but what is at the back of the back stage. But I have another question:

would you regard a counter clerk in a travel agency as a manager, on the grounds that she is all the time dealing with human beings by serving them?'

'Perhaps you are trying to catch me out, HC! In this instance we don't reckon she is a manager as most of her work and function consists in exchanging knowledge and experience. This is reckoned as a technical function though we should always value the skill of dealing with other human beings, as with the barista. In one sense you could say her knowledge and experience are almost equivalent to those of a machine or a device which is storing memory.'

## The principle of negation: what management is not—a non-technical function at its core

'So: can we agree on this? The job of a manager is non-technical. It does not consist of doing the technical work though he or she must have a high level understanding of technical work. Think of the conductor of an orchestra. The conductor doesn't play an instrument, but guides the whole interpretation of the piece, balancing different sections of the orchestra and individual instruments. The conductor is not a player but must have a good sense of where the music is going; the conductor must also be an excellent listener. Nothing must escape his or her ear.'

'And this surely relates to something you've often talked about, which is "the feel"?'

'Yes, absolutely. There's a story about the famous Austrian conductor Herbert von Karajan. Apparently Karajan once stopped a rehearsal because he heard something was not quite right. In fact one of the violinists in the orchestra had a sore wrist. Karajan slowed the tempo to accommodate the injured player. Later we will discuss someone we both admire, the tennis player Roger Federer. I think we both agree that one of many things that make Federer's game extraordinary is his feel: it seems Federer can somehow "feel" what is happening on the other side of the net even when he has his back turned.'

## Management is not a noun but a verb in the active present

'Have you noticed,' continues GP, 'how often we are confused by the limitations of language and grammar themselves? We assume that the word is the thing, the description is the thing described. But we may be wrong about that. For instance, 'management' is not really a thing, not really a noun though grammatically so. In the 1980s Harold Geneen, who had been the successful CEO of the American conglomerate ITT, wrote a book on management and called it 'Managing'. The book appealed to managers because it captured something essential about the spirit of management: it is not a thing, but a process, a verb in the active present. Management consists of managing, day to day, hour to hour, minute to minute. This is at the heart of understanding the state of mind which is ever dynamic and in the moment. This understanding is moment-to-moment, like having your finger on the pulse: it is also what we can call the feel. This feel is ever present and not based on working hours—be they 40 hours or 70 hours a week.'

That seems a good point at which to pause. We have an early start next day and I need to get back to the hotel to pack and prepare for the road trip. I'm beginning to see that management is a deeper, but also more deeply human, subject than I ever realized.

# 6

# Understanding Operations of the Mind

## *Core of management*

---

My day starts with a morning swim. There's a rooftop pool, surrounded by trees, with curious birds but no other swimmers. I swim a few lengths, shaking off some of the stiffness of travel. Swimming is the best way to clear the mind, I've always found. Something elemental about being in the water, which goes back to earliest times—maybe even species memory, of the time when water was our element, before our ancestors crawled out of the ocean onto the land.

I have breakfast, where there is almost too much choice, and too many waiters being attentive. I feel churlish complaining about this but what I want at this moment is to be left alone. Actually this could be relevant to what GP and I have been discussing. No doubt these waiters have been highly trained and they have a professional air. But what they lack is 'the feel'. After breakfast I check out. I wait in the lobby for GP.

Our idea is to set off early, to miss the worst of the commuter traffic, head down to the south, towards the village and the great central southern city. As I expect, GP appears, absolutely on time. 'Ready to go?'

We don't miss all the traffic, but we can continue the conversation from the previous evening.

'I feel we've only scratched the surface, so far, HC.'

'Well, perhaps we've made some progress in defining what management is not, using the tool of negation. It's not doing, in the technical sense. It has to do with dealing with other people.'

'Yes, yes,' said GP, sounding a little impatient. 'But what aspect of other people.'

'That's a good question. Their characters, habitual behaviours, interactions. What makes them tick, I suppose.'

'And how do we learn that?'

There's a pause. Then the figure of Panna with the empty space on the bench next to him on the dashboard begins to vibrate slightly. A voice is heard. It is Panna speaking.

'Do you two really know what you are talking about?'

Panna sounds somewhat irritated. 'Are you asking the right question? Because if you don't ask the right question, you certainly will not arrive at the right answer. A right question which will also awaken our own native intelligence. You speak of understanding the operations of the mind of others. How is it possible unless you are able to understand the operations of your own mind?'

GP and I look at each other. Eventually, GP responds, 'Say more.'

'You see you all want to learn from others; please don't. Especially when it comes to understanding the operations of the mind, which essentially form the consciousness or the whole psychological structure of the human being. First of all you must observe your own minds, and your own hearts, and your own existence, your daily life as you live it. You learn about yourself in the mirror of relationship. The relationship you have with everything around you. No learning from others when it comes to the psychological realm: this is the core of management.'

There's a pause as we try to take in what Panna has just said. The last straggly outskirts of the city are giving way to open countryside.

Finally GP resumes. 'Have you heard of Tom Watson, HC?'

'Not the golfer?

'No, the Founding Chairman and CEO of IBM. Quite a remarkable man in his way. He said that we must study through reading, listening, discussing, observing, and thinking. These are very good things. Listening. Observing. Thinking. I don't know what Tom Watson meant or how he went about explaining what he meant. All these are part of the core of management which we will be talking over together throughout.'

Now we are finally clear of the outskirts of the great city. We are proceeding south, over a parched red plateau, with distant hills visible on both sides. Though it's very dry here, especially at this season, there is some cultivation, of citrus fruits and nuts.

## Art of Listening—Listening to the Book of Yourself

I am about to suggest some music from the sound system when the figure on the dashboard speaks again.

'What you must read is not the book of numbers, which many tech entrepreneurs are caught up with, but the book of yourself. That means you must have the art of listening to what the book is saying. Listening doesn't mean interpreting.'

'I guess the art of listening isn't so simple,' mutters GP.

'Oh no, not simple at all,' laughs Panna. 'Or perhaps it is simple, when one has gone through all the complexity of it.'

'Just observe it as you would observe a cloud. You can't have any effect on the cloud, or the palm leaves swaying in the wind, or the beauty of the sunset; you can't alter it. So one must have the art of listening to what the book is saying. The book is you; it will reveal everything.'

*– Friend on the Bench*[1]

There is a long pause. We pass through a small town, hardly more than a village. Eventually GP offers this: 'Let's say that the listening and observing we are talking about is not just casual seeing, or external seeing: seeing a leaf without observing its structure of veins, its shapeliness, or a cloud without appreciating the light shining through it, or crossing a stream and not hearing the murmur of the water. We are talking about being able to observe yourself without denial or over-easy acceptance, as you really are—not to be afraid or ashamed of that. To see yourself as part of the whole; to see yourself without your own shadow coming in the way.'

Suddenly the traffic, which has been proceeding quite smoothly, bunches up; people flash their warning lights; everything grinds to a halt.

Our first thought is that there's been an accident. But minutes go past and nothing moves. One or two drivers are getting out of their cars to see what is causing the stoppage. I follow suit. But there's nothing to be seen; just an unexplained jam.

There's nothing to be done, apparently. Or is there?

GP's mind moves faster than mine. He is on the phone to someone, a friend in the next town where we are planning to stop for lunch. Information is coming through: the block has been caused by farmers who are protesting about a delayed land reform. They have dumped hundreds of tons of produce on the carriageway and they are sitting down, refusing to move.

It's a muddle really. The farmers have a justified issue. We are caught up in someone else's conflict. Some drivers are very impatient and horns are honking. GP and I get out of the car and sit on a raised bank between the two carriageways.

'I suppose we have to admit we're stuck, for the moment, and there's nothing much we can do about it. No point in getting upset about it. No point in honking horns,' I finally offer.

'When you say, 'I know hunger', you have directly experienced it; but the man who has never experienced hunger can also say, 'I know hunger'. The two states of 'knowing' are entirely different, the one is direct experience and the other is descriptive knowledge.'

– *Friend on the Bench*[2]

'There is all the difference between being told what an astounding thing the mind is and making the discovery for yourself. The two states are entirely different.'

– *Friend on the Bench*[3]

'Maybe you're wiser than me, HC. I was thinking of actions we could take, maybe turning back and finding another route, if we could get onto the other carriageway.'

'It looks like we can't.'

GP's expression relaxes and he smiles. 'This is actually a good illustration of what we were talking about. Understanding the operations of the mind.

'Just now I suppose we were both wondering what we could do, if there was some way we could escape from this situation. All kinds of thoughts were whirring through my brain—I don't know about yours. How we could get more information. How we could alert the authorities. And so on. Perhaps in the end there's nothing we can do. In this case it's beyond our control.'

We get back into the car. To while away the time GP plays Heart of Gold by Neil Young on the sound system.

'I want to live
I want to give
I've been a miner
For a heart of gold
That keeps me searching?
For a heart of gold
…'

'I love this song,' I comment.

'Yes. What Neil Young is saying is very relevant. Especially for those working in the tech field. It might bring awareness that you also have to search for something inside yourself, besides always searching on the internet and mining data in the office.'

And now, just as suddenly as it started, the jam is loosening. There is movement ahead. Soon we are approaching the medium-sized town where we are to have lunch with a friend of GP's.

GP's old college friend CF runs a chain of cinemas in the town and, after we explain the delay caused by the road-block, proudly shows us round one. It's a sleek modern-looking place with several

'We do not know the workings of our own mind — the mind as it is, not as it should be or as we would like it to be. The mind is the only instrument we have, the instrument with which we think, what we act, in which we have our being.'

*- Friend on the Bench*[4]

screens, clearly popular among the younger generation. At his home a traditional meal is served; the women of the house do not just do all the preparing and cooking but also do the serving.

Back in the car, on the last leg of the day's run, we think back over the day's conversation and experience.

## Need to understand the operations of the mind

GP summarizes where we've got to. 'We've established that at the core of management is the need to understand the operations of the mind, and to observe our own mind in action. But do we know what is meant by 'mind'? By the way people use these words, mind, brain, consciousness somewhat indiscriminately; they have no doubt given all kinds of problems to philosophers.

'And we should make clear we are not teaching core of management to anybody as it is not something that can be taught. Core of management cannot be taught but it can be learnt. In that sense it's much like hunger: whatever way I describe it, still it is only a description and that description is not hunger. You have to feel it yourself.'

'Yes, that makes sense, as our friend the guide said.'

## What is mind ?

'Back to fundamentals. In management, to deal with fellow managers or colleagues, it is imperative to understand them. How can a manager who has no understanding of himself understand others? Understanding oneself is understanding the workings of mind. You don't use a defective testing instrument to measure the quality of other instruments. The truth of the matter is that mind and me are not two different entities. We have to understand the entity 'Manager' is nothing but the manager's mind.'

## Understanding Mind

'So, as we were saying earlier, how do we understand 'mind'?'

'I think we can agree it is required that one understands oneself directly and not through an intermediary. So the focus must obviously be on direct experience. It is important to keep in view that direct experience owes nothing to any authority—it's not about following anybody however venerable they are, imitating anybody or any outside influence, compulsion. This needs to be a spontaneous process.'

There is a rumbling and whirring from the car dashboard. Panna has decided to chip in. 'We can't have a method or technique to understand mind. The best word I can use is 'framework' which essentially provides an approach. But please don't mistake this word 'framework' to imply mind is a frozen entity. Mind is a living and dynamic thing. I am using this word just to explain. It is like telling your friend that he can reach your home by a two-wheeler. How your friend rides his two-wheeler is up to him.'

## Outer world and inner world.

GP becomes quite impassioned. 'In this framework of the mind of human beings there are two worlds—outer and inner. We could also use different words to describe these two worlds–as physical domain and psychological domain. Let us stick to the expressions—physical domain and psychological domain. Inner world is the psychological domain or consciousness which is synonymous with the mind.

'Conventionally speaking one thinks these worlds are two different worlds and apart from each other. In reality they are not two separate entities but one integrated whole. First you see the outer things and from there go inward, watch how the mind is responding to the outer. This going inward from outward is the thread of relationship that exists between the two. The awareness of existence of this thread is the integrating factor of these two

'If we do not understand that mind in operation as it is functioning in each one of us, any problem that we are confronted with will become more complex and more destructive. So, it seems to me, to understand one's mind is the first essential function of all education.'

*– Friend on the Bench*[5]

'If you do not understand yourself, you will not understand anything else; you may have great ideals, beliefs, and formulations, but they will have no reality. They will be delusions.'

– *Friend on the Bench*[6]

apparently different worlds. This awareness is from moment to moment and exists throughout one's life. We are not prescribing any method here but simply stating what is happening. If you need to understand this, you have to experience it yourself.'

## Mind and State of mind

Once again Panna intervenes. 'The real challenge is that one should find out for oneself what this extraordinary thing called the mind is, because it is the mind that creates the problems. If one can understand the way problems arise in one's mind, one needs to check if that understanding is a way of balancing the affairs. Mind is not a static entity. It is always moving. Understanding the mind is about understanding the state of mind. The dynamic aspect of the mind, that is the state of mind which could be different from moment to moment, as against the static state. The static state can be understood in retrospect, which has its own limitations. Mind in operation as it is operating in the moment is what has significance.

'When one gets angry, one thinks of managing the anger and tries various methods in managing one's anger, or goes to an Anger Manager. All this implies that one is different from one's anger. In reality are they two different entities or are they one? When one gets angry one is not different from the anger. In fact one is the anger. This realization that one is not separate from anger could be the real beginning of managing one's anger. For a manager this is so vital as the manager has to deal with his colleagues and subordinates—that means the actions, reactions and provocations of working with people.'

There is a pause. Panna's voice goes quiet. He has given us much to chew over.

GP eventually intervenes. 'I recall that Harold Geneen, former CEO of ITT, said in his book *Managing*, "it is not alcoholism that is the enemy of the manager but it is egotism".'

'So you must know yourself to understand the present and through the present, the past. From the known present, the hidden layers of the past are discovered and this discovery is liberating and creative.'

– *Friend on the Bench*[7]

Panna resumed. 'Exactly right. The enemy is not the other, it is you.'

'And human beings have accepted this egoism as an inevitable part of human existence. This has become the major problem or the only problem psychologically speaking. To understand the ego we have to understand our own consciousness which creates this ego. They are not two separate entities.'

There is another pause. 'We are not lecturing to anyone, remember,' Panna resumes. 'What the Friend on the Bench does is to make observations of what is actually taking place outside, in the world, and inside, in the mind. But these observations are devoid of personal prejudices, preconceptions, and motives. All are statements of facts. In that sense he is a true master of reality. It is up to the listener to see if the statement is valid or not. Certainly, he is not trying to convince you of anything.

'So when we say 'mind', we mean 'the brain, the movement of thought, the experiences accumulated as knowledge, memory, the whole momentum of thinking, and the senses': all that is the mind, which is essentially consciousness. This is what I can say, to communicate conventionally speaking.'

'The mind sounds quite a complex thing,' I offer.

'Many-layered.'

'And if the mind is not aware of itself, of the extraordinary complexities, merely concentrating on any detail, on one particularity, will destroy the totality.'

– *Friend on the Bench*[8]

# 7

# Result of Time

## *Time and conditioning*

GP goes quiet. He seems to be thinking. 'Oh yes,' continues the voice of Panna from the dashboard. 'Layer after layer. Going back thousands of years, from the most primitive instincts, of fear of predators for instance, through all the layers of culture and history. All these are present in the mind. The mind has accumulated an immense mass of knowledge, technology and so on. But we have to be aware of the totality of the mind, not just one aspect or detail. Human minds are conditioned. So the responses are conditioned and manifestations that occur are only extensions of this conditioning.'

'But if one is aware of one's conditioning,' I offer, 'that awareness may put the conditioning in a certain perspective.'

### Centuries of conditioning and result of time

Panna sounds serious. 'But we really need to go into the depths of this conditioning. For centuries we have been conditioned by all sorts of things, our nationality, caste, class, the language we happen to speak, the culture, tradition, religion we are brought up in, received ideas of all kinds. Then there are very practical and basic things, the type of food we eat, the climate we live in. We are all tremendously influenced by our parents, aren't we? Friends and experiences also come into it. So we have to be aware that our responses to every situation are conditioned. But are we aware that we are conditioned? Are you aware that you are conditioned? That is what you've got to ask yourself, rather than how to be free of your conditioning. The fact is that you may never be free of it. You may start saying 'I must be free of my conditioning', then that becomes another trap, because it's about what you'd like to be the case, not what is the case.'

'Can we be free of this conditioning?' I ask. 'Or are we going to be dictated by our conditioning always?'

Suddenly GP has a thought. 'Even computers and smart phones are conditioned, in their case by all their preloaded software, operating systems, and those themselves have evolved over decades.'

## The deeper conditioning

Panna has more to say. 'It's not just that we may not be free of our conditioning. We may not even be aware of all the levels of it. These are deeper level factors race, caste, language, religion etc. and also at the individual level. Many people show an aggression in their attitude to life they may not even be aware of.'

'I'm not sure I understand,' I put in. 'What do you mean by this?'

'I mean that aggression takes many forms. It could be seeking dominance, or power or status. It's so difficult to be free of that, because it operates at a very subtle level. And a person may think he or she is not aggressive, not at all, quite the opposite, because they appear superficially mild or gentle. But such a person may have an ideal they are deeply wedded to, and they can't let go of.

'Our minds, brains are very, very, very old, it is not something new that we have acquired when you are born, it is a tremendously old mind heavily conditioned to occupy itself with itself.'

– *Friend on the Bench*[1]

'If one is brought up in childhood in an environment where one's family has a strongly right-wing outlook it can happen that one also acquires a right-wing outlook in life. How does one look at a guru in robes of a particular religion? One may go close to him or one may shy away from him. Probably this could be due to the influences operating within oneself. Right-wing influences could draw one nearer to the robed guru and left-wing influences could repel one from the robed guru. This is how normally things happen, a very clear binary mode. It implies that one needs to transcend both left-wing influences and right-wing influences if one has understood the underlying truth of the matter.'

'To sum up,' GP intervenes, 'I'm conditioned to act or react in a certain way in part because I belong to a certain culture, or religion, brought up in a certain geography with its own climatic conditions, clothing, food or culture, or because I adhere to a particular ideology.'

'Like your friend CF,' I put in. 'He comes from quite a traditional background, in which women are expected to do the housework and cooking. There's the influence of our parents, our schools, our background. Our culture and history. Religion. Language. In my case as you know I was brought up as a Catholic. Later I rejected the dogmas of Catholicism but I am sure I am marked by it. Much of it seemed to be about being special, either persecuted or superior or both. But I didn't feel superior to my father, who was an atheist.'

Panna has not gone away. 'And do you think it's so easy to spot this conditioning, to really be aware of it? Are you free of your Catholic conditioning, HC? Or you, GP, of your political conditioning?'

'They talk about Catholic guilt as something that marks you forever,' I ponder.

'You have to be aware that the mind is being influenced all the time to think along certain lines,' continues Panna. 'Once upon a time it was the religions that had the most influence—you mention

'I am the result of the past, of innumerable layers of the past, of a series of causes-effects. And how can I be opposed to the whole, the past, when I am the result of all that?'

— *Friend on the Bench*[2]

your Catholic upbringing. Now the governments have taken over. And don't think it's just the Communists or the Fascists. They all want to shape and control your mind. Including the capitalists! I had experience of all of them. Maybe on the surface you think you can resist their control. You think you have worked it all out, thought it all through. But that's just on the surface, isn't it? Below the surface, in the deep unconscious, there are all these other influences, the whole weight of history, of tradition, urging you in a particular direction. And deep down below the surface, in the unconscious, your ambitions, your unsolved problems, your compulsions, superstitions, fears, are waiting, throbbing, urging.'

We've been driving for a few hours now. The landscape doesn't change much; the high red plateau with its distant hills and mountains seems almost endless. Sometimes I can see a bird of prey circling high above us. But now we are approaching another town; more cultivation, citrus orchards, appear. There are stalls selling fresh fruit and vegetables by the side of the road. We buy some guavas which are fresh and delicious, especially after the long hot journey. We decide to get out of the car, stretch our legs, take a breather.

We are back in the car, and the figure of Panna begins to whir and rumble. 'We are on a car journey, and we can use car driving as an analogy of what we are talking about, understanding the workings of the mind, awareness, attention.'

'Say more, Panna. I am not sure I follow.'

'Put it like this. If you are starting off on your journey in your car, don't you think you should understand the level of fuel in the tank, the condition of the basic things like brakes, accelerator and the steering wheel, not to mention the timely servicing of the car in a workshop and the ability to drive the car?'

'Of course.'

'And as you start driving the car and once you are on the road, the most important factor is paying attention to driving which exists only in the moment. Let us assume that all the basic things are in order, and you have a capable driver. Similar to your journey by the car, can we say that the journey of life also needs to begin with this kind of understanding of what is near?'

'I think I follow but carry on.'

'The 'near' is your mind. There's an assumption that one understands what the mind is and how it operates. Understanding mind obviously implies understanding the process of thought. We all know that thought is the basic instrument of our life. Conventionally one tends to think that there are only thoughts and emotions that form the basis of living. I doubt if most of us ever wonder that there may be something else other than thought as the instrument of living.'

'Are you saying there is?'

'Yes, I am. This something else is 'awareness' and 'awareness' is not thought. How do we distinguish awareness from thought?'

'I have a vague sense they are different but explain further.'

'Let us continue with the example of car driving. Do we know whether the mind also has an accelerator and brakes like a car? How many people are applying the accelerator or applying the brakes when required? Are they aware of this in the first place when it comes to mind? Or do they carry on without being aware, applying the brakes in place of the accelerator? Or applying both brakes and accelerator at the same time? What happens when you apply both brakes and accelerator at the same time?'

'There's a horrible screeching sound, and you're going to strain and stress the engine.'

'Yes, the friction will quickly lead to the engine seizing up. Similarly the mind, which is the basic instrument of life, could also suffer wear and tear when subject to contradiction and conflict. One has so many desires, one opposed to the other. It is obvious that pursuit of these contradictory desires results in friction in the mind. The fundamental question is whether one knows that there is awareness, which has its own action, quite separate from mind, existing in itself.

'Let us take another example like sitting on the floor. If one is aware of the way one is sitting on the floor, one automatically straightens one's back to a straight posture. One does that without thinking. Similarly, if you're aware when driving the car and you're making a quick turn to the right, you automatically apply the brakes and not the accelerator. One has to understand this quality of awareness has some distinct properties. Firstly, it exists in the moment only. It is non-accumulative. One might have driven a car for thirty years. But on day one of the thirty-first year one still has to remain attentive. One's past experience of paying attention is of no use on that day. In that sense awareness and attention can be classified as one and the same or belonging to the same level or class in the language of software programming. We also use the words 'understanding' and 'intelligence' in the same sense throughout our book. The factor of 'feel' is part of this understanding. If you stick your fingers in an electric plug, you will get an electric shock. This statement can be understood either intellectually or in a real way. We keep referring to awareness, attention, understanding, intelligence and the expression 'the feel' in this real sense.

'The second most important factor of awareness is that it has its own action: it is never the case that you first become aware and then you act. In that sense awareness is action. Or you can say attention or understanding is action. This is the truth of the matter psychologically speaking. It is instantaneous. But the physical action obviously takes time.

# 8

# Vulnerability

*To be vulnerable is to live*

---

'Another extremely important aspect of attention', resumes Panna, 'is vulnerability of the mind. Vulnerability does not mean fear—being scared or being afraid or becoming paranoid. Vulnerability is not taking things for granted. If you take the example of car driving you must be neither overconfident nor reckless while driving. Both states, in the end, have the same effect: they result from the mind not being truly alert. On the other hand, if one is attentive one can remain sane while driving. This attentiveness or caution is what can be called vulnerability. It is vulnerability that makes the mind attentive. In fact this vulnerability is the essential component of sane living and not taking things for granted.'

There is a pause while GP and I take this in. 'That's interesting,' I reflect. 'Many people want to avoid being or seeming vulnerable as it seems to imply weakness. But you're saying, in a sense, it's the opposite.'

## To be vulnerable is to live

'Exactly,' agrees Panna. 'But now I want to discuss something else. We were talking about the accelerator of the car. How do we understand that in the case of mind? Thought has the quality of speed. Some time back Microsoft used a tagline 'At the speed of thought' in its advertisements. In the case of mind there are also responses to the sensations. These responses are in the form of thoughts. These responses depend on the conditioning of the mind. We can say the accelerator of the mind is the effect of the responses of the mind which are essentially thoughts and emotions. We don't seem to realize that thought quickly takes over the sensations much like in an Olympic relay race and thus we are unaware of the moment when this handing over of the baton takes place, from senses to thought. Mind is unaware of the moment the baton gets exchanged. It is only a tiny fraction of a second. But the fact is that the mind is unaware.'

'I think I get all that. It makes me think of the speed of light. Light travels extraordinarily fast but it does travel in time. So there is a gap between transmitter and receiver. So, in the case of mind, what could be the brakes?'

GP chips in. 'Ah it is here that the most important level of human existence comes into play. That is to say, awareness—which could come into play in the most natural way and act automatically in the same way that the driver, if he or she is aware, applies the brakes automatically, or lets the car run on. Then it's a case of letting the action go forward spontaneously. One needs to check this out personally oneself.'

## No separation

'And if you're thinking of the hard disk in a computer, the system and system administrator are two separate entities. A corrupted hard disc gets formatted by the System Administrator so that you can start working on the system that is refreshed.'

'I believe that is so—you are right GP. But when it comes to understanding the corruption of the mind, there are no two separate entities, as in me and my mind. There is only the state of understanding, and both the separate entities disappear. If one realizes or understands the corruption of the mind in the true sense, one becomes the system and also the system administrator. This very understanding has its own action which refreshes the mind naturally. This understanding implies deep honesty—the ability to see things as they are. Mind in a state of confusion has to admit to itself that it is confused—that is, to see its own confusion. This very understanding has its own action which refreshes the mind naturally. So it is the realization or understanding that there are no two separate entities that is the beginning of bringing some clarity or some functional order.'

GP and I reflect on what Panna has said. Then I ask a question: 'What happens when a manager has to show anger to deal with a colleague or team member? If he is soft and 'goody-goody' he may not achieve the result. What do you think Panna?'

'Awareness in the moment is the key', Panna replies. 'If the manager is aware of the anger that is arising in the manager, that is himself, he can easily check himself and will not resort to any violent act. The best he can do is continue his expression of anger as that may have some positive effect on the colleague. Be aware, but not be in caught in it.'

Finally, it seems, Panna has come to the end of his long disquisition. We carry on driving for a while, until we reach a town of some size, a district capital. The town is fairly nondescript. GP has booked us a hotel in the centre, where there's a bustle of street markets and traders. We're pleased to arrive and settle, and arrange to have a simple meal in the hotel restaurant.

'So we're in the middle of the journey, GP,' I begin as we sit down to eat. 'And as Dante said at the beginning of the Inferno, we seem to be in a dark wood. Things aren't clear at all. In fact they seem to have become more complex. We're deep in the thickets of the mind, it appears.'

GP looks thoughtful. We're both quite hungry, it appears. The restaurant's speciality is an excellent biryani. After a while he breaks the silence. 'Who are we, HC?'

I ponder the question GP has posed.

'You could say we are made up of layers, like an onion, as I think you suggested a while back. There's the outer layer, our name, our job title, our qualifications, our identity. In your case you are an entrepreneur, who is now involved in work concerning the work of the Institutions left behind by the Friend on the Bench. I am a writer who has published a few books and hundreds of articles. You studied accountancy. I went to a well-known university.'

## The conscious, the unconscious, and conditioning

'We could put it like this. Many people, including psychologists, have talked about the conscious mind and the unconscious mind. The conscious mind is occupied with the everyday duties — it observes, thinks, argues, attends to a job, and so on. But are we aware of the unconscious mind?'

'Almost by definition we can't be.'

'Right. The unconscious mind is the repository of instinct, it is the residue of this or that civilization, of this or that culture, in which there are certain urges, various forms of compulsion. And can this whole mind, the unconscious as well as the conscious, uncondition itself?'

'I guess it's difficult for the unconscious mind to uncondition itself if it is unconscious.'

'Right again. So why do we divide mind as the conscious and the unconscious? Is there such a definite barrier between the conscious and the unconscious mind? Or are we so taken up with the conscious mind that we have never considered or been open to the unconscious? And can the conscious mind investigate, probe into the unconscious, or is it only when the conscious mind is quiet that the unconscious promptings, hints, urges, compulsions come into being?'

'I think the conscious mind is a bit like a dictator—it has a tendency to take over and control everything. It has to let go a little.'

'I agree. It is a total process which comes about with the earnest intention to find out if your mind is conditioned.

'We've already spoken of how the mind is conditioned by all these factors, some external such as climate, others to do with culture and ideology (capitalism as much as communism!), religion and so on.

'If we do not like to use these two words conscious and unconscious, we might use the terms superficial and the hidden, the superficial parts of the mind and the deeper layers of the mind. The whole of the conscious as well as the unconscious, the superficial as well as the hidden, the total process of our thinking—only part of which we are conscious of, and the rest which is the major part we are not conscious of—is what we call consciousness. This is the result of centuries of man's endeavour.

'So if the manager's job is dealing with people, he or she must understand what makes them tick, not only externally but internally. Dealing with the qualifications or skillsets which are manifested outwardly is not so difficult. If someone is qualified in Chartered Accountancy they can be put in the finance section. This is the easy part. Dealing with the inner world of a person is the real challenge. How do you go about engaging with these factors which constitute the inner world, which is essentially the human mind?'

There's a pause. People are leaving the restaurant and heading home. We are both tired and decide to turn in for the night.

# 9

# Brain and Computer

## *The analogy*

---

Over breakfast—dosa again—I decide to fly a kite, in the interests of trying to see how to go about understanding the inner workings of a human being: that is to say, the human mind. 'Nowadays when people talk about the human mind, or the brain, they very often use the analogy of the computer, don't they? They talk about hardware and software, being hardwired to do this or that, or being programmed—maybe we could pursue this as we drive down today, see where it takes us?'

'That's a good idea HC. We can make use of this analogy—though I think we'll see it has its limitations—as the computer is the closest thing humans have invented to replace the work of their brain. And also, nowadays especially with the evolution of AI, nearly everyone throughout the world uses computers and/or smart phones. That may make the comparison easier to understand. Sometimes people compare the physical brain to the hardware of the computer or phone and thinking to the software. Understanding the process of thinking is as important in life—or more important!—as understanding the workings of a computer.

'Let us say that most of the users of computers know how to create and store documents. Some of them may be familiar with these software applications at work—for example MS Word for creating and storing documents (also stored as .doc) and PDF for documents in pdf format (also stored as .pdf).'

'Yes, I expect so, though I don't know how to create a pdf. But carry on.'

'On the other hand, most users of computers and smartphones may not be aware or may not have any interest in understanding the underlying Operating System (OS) and its functionalities.'

'Certainly that is the case for me, GP!'

'Well, if you don't mind me lecturing a bit, I can explain that there are three major Operating Systems that are driving nearly all computers and the technology evolution today. Windows OS, Linux and Mac OS. Though software applications (like Word and pdf) are written by software programmers and are within the knowledge of most of the users, users are probably not aware of the overall controls the OS imposes on the programmers and the applications they develop.'

'Explain further. I am listening.'

'For instance the operating system—OS—lays down the protocols regarding the flow of data. Similarly it provides security controls, libraries etc. So no application can violate the overall constraints the OS imposes. These are only a few examples just for illustration.

'And just to provide some more knowledge about the way software works: we can say that a programmer develops an application using a programming language like C++ or Java or something else. This language is readable by human beings, though only a software programmer can understand it. But for the computer to work according to this programme, the programmer has to convert his source code into another format for a computer to read and work with it. This format is binaries which are also called executables. This format essentially consists of zeros and ones and hence is readable by a machine.'

'All clear so far.'

'So now let us further explore the functioning of a computer to understand the workings of the human mind. Nearly all computer users have encountered glitches sometimes while working. If a document, worked very diligently, appears distorted when retrieved from the disk the user obviously gets flustered. But when the software programmer who has written the source code encounters the same glitch, it may not upset him, because he has the knowledge of the source code and which in turn can tell him why and how the glitch is occurring.'

'So, GP, could we say that the challenge is this? As in the case of a glitch and the source code writer, is it possible for a manager to remain calm as he or she deals with a troublesome situation in his team?'

'Well said, HC. That implies starting with the outer manifestation of the issue at hand, and then from there going inward to get a deeper understanding of the issue. As we explained about the OS of a computer being the hidden layer of its workings, it appears the religious conditioning of the mind is part of the hidden layers of the mind. Other factors like culture, climate, nationality also contribute to the hidden layers of conditioning of the mind.'

We have crossed from one state to another but the landscape hasn't changed much. Still the red earth, the clear blue sky, and distant hills. So much has come out of this land, religions, languages, different states and rulers; the land endures, harsh but beautiful, dry most of the year except for the monsoon season when the dry river beds fill and overflow. In the immense perspectives of time and space, one human life can feel quite small and insignificant.

There's a rumble from the figure on the dashboard. It seems Panna has been paying attention to the conversation.

'Today Artificial Intelligence is the buzzword. A good thing it is called 'artificial'; at least we can preserve the word 'intelligence' for the natural intelligence of human beings. It's that natural intelligence that a manager has to use in his day-to-day function of dealing with this team and colleagues.

'The point is that it's the current state of mind or *quality* of mind as the manager is going through the various situations from day to day that he or she needs to be aware of. This awareness or understanding is the non-technical component which is at the heart of management, and we can call this *core of management*: now this is completely different from the operation of a computer or a mechanical way of living.'

'I agree,' responds GP. 'But can you explain how?'

'First let me make this point: Whatever I say is my understanding of what the Friend on the Bench said.

'So the understanding or awareness of one's state of mind from moment to moment can be called self-knowing, whereas the knowledge of the state of mind in the past can be called self-knowledge. Self-knowing is intimately connected to 'the feel' that is so essential in managing people. Observing the way the mind is responding and relating to various situations and things, both inside and outside, from moment to moment, is the essence of self-knowing. It is non-accumulative—like the attention you pay when driving a car.

'Without this self-knowing a manager or an entrepreneur is like a blind person moving along the journey without being aware he or she is blind.'

There is a long pause. Panna appears to have returned to his own realm. Silence holds sway in the car. We've been driving for many hours and the sun is just beginning to fall away towards the west, though there is little change in the landscape.

I haven't really been thinking about the route we are taking, and it strikes me we haven't discussed where we are spending the night.

The landscape begins to look familiar to me. There are big red hills, and we are entering a valley, more thickly wooded than most of the rest of the dry plateau. GP turns off the main road and we proceed along a quite narrow but well-paved side road before arriving at what looks like the entrance to a campus.

Suddenly it dawns on me. 'This is the School in the Valley!' GP smiles.

I'm back at the School where I studied for a few years as a young kid, before my family took off on its rootless wanderings to California and Britain. Not only that, this is the School founded by that mysterious man the Friend on the Bench, whom Panna refers to as the Master of Reality.

I haven't returned to this place for decades but gradually memories seep back to me.

We come to a courtyard whose centrepiece is a great spreading banyan tree, with many taproots; a tree so voluminous it is like a small forest all on its own. A little further on is a modest two-storey white house. 'Ah, that was the Friend on the Bench's house. He was no longer there but one room had been left the way he furnished it, very simply. Another room was the Library.'

'It still is,' said GP.

We proceed a little further, and reach a small clearing, backing onto woods, with what look like two double huts.

'These have been built since you were last here, HC. This is the new visitors' accommodation.'

GP shows me to my accommodation—he obviously knows the ropes here. 'You can unpack and wash if you like. And then if you feel up to it we can play tennis.'

Now I know why GP suggested that I pack my tennis gear.

The courts are quite a walk away, on the far side of the campus. They're part of a large expanse of sports grounds. As we walk over we pass a few students returning from games.

The courts are hard courts with blue coating on the surface. The exercise livens us up after many hours in the car.

The game is over. It's now quite late in the day, towards sundown. In the golden light, the ancient weathered rocks of the surrounding hills with their sparse vegetation are glowing red and purple; noisy flocks of birds are gathering in preparation for the evening roost. We're sitting on a bench beside the two tennis courts. A dog, looking perhaps more for company than food, sidles up and lies down beside us. Everything, for the moment at least, feels calm and serene.

'When you play a shot in tennis,' I venture, 'you have to be in the moment. Aware of your quality of mind if you like. As soon as you start thinking ahead of yourself, or obsessing about some shot you've missed, you're lost.'

'You're just crafty,' laughs GP.

# 10

# Work-Life Balance

## *Coffee darshan, a pause in the day*

---

After our game of tennis, GP and I retire briefly to the guest quarters. Big windows give out onto a terrace, with tables for sitting; a lawn and beyond that the forest. It is a tranquil, lovely place, perfect for a reflective break from hectic activity. The birds, though, are busy, calling to one another, hopping around in the branches, venturing onto the lawn.

We have a dinner invitation, it turns out, with the former Director along with her colleague who has a doctorate in physics and is a senior administrator of the school. She is also an Indologist and conservationist, married to a philosopher, a quiet smiling man who says little but seems to take in much. All three have dedicated their lives to the wellbeing of the School, and indeed the whole valley and its neighbourhood. We discuss the challenges of maintaining the founding aims and principles of the school, that education should not be primarily about instilling technical knowledge or facility but about nurturing the development of a child as a whole human being, often against the demands of parents and others in a competitive world.

'The place itself must have the quality of being inspiring,' she tells us. 'That means the natural environment as well as or more than the school buildings. We learn from nature more than anything, and from time outside the classroom probably more than from time in the classroom.'

The school has engaged in a remarkable programme of reforestation and 'greening' of what used to be a somewhat dry and dusty expanse. Formerly bare hillsides are now green with young trees. In the valley where the school is set, bare weathered rocks, shaped fortuitously into the likeness of animals, rise up from a verdant valley floor of low shrubs and taller trees.

'It wasn't easy, you know,' explains the former Director. 'We are responsible for reforestation of a large area of what is now the campus. But that was only the beginning. We needed to exclude grazing animals, which simply eat up all the young shoots, and at first it was a challenge to explain our rationale to the local farmers. But then, thirty-five years ago, there was a sequence of drought years and they began to see the advantages of re-greening the valley and the hillsides. We created two lakes. I am happy with what we have done but there is always more to do.'

I chip in. 'I've just read that the whole area has now been declared a bird reserve and more than 200 species have been observed.'

'If you like,' the former Director tells me, as we move to the table where an array of beautifully fresh-looking vegetable curry dishes, rice, chutneys and raithas is laid out, 'you can go out on the morning bird-watching walk tomorrow.'

'I'd be delighted,' I reply.

'It starts at 5.30 am, by the way. To catch the dawn chorus and activity, before the birds settle down and the heat rises.'

I rise early, before it's fully light. It's cool in the early mornings here and I need a jacket. I'm joined in the main courtyard of the school by two other bird enthusiasts, a teacher and a parent of one of the pupils. Both are far more expert and prepared—with powerful binoculars, phone apps and so on—than I am. The parent seems to have a list of species and is keen to tick off the ones he hasn't yet identified.

I decide to take a different approach. I suddenly remember some words of the Friend on the Bench. He spoke of how if you go into some wild place and remain still for a while, the birds and animals will begin to accept you and lose their shyness. They will even come to you. He even said one could hear the roots of the trees growing. I find by remaining still I see so much more; there is activity among the trees, and a quail-like bird emerges from among the rocks. There is so much variety of bird life here. Each species speaks its own language. There is one bird of particular beauty, with a blue head, chestnut body and impossibly long slender tail; I later learn that this is the male paradise flycatcher.

I get back to our guest quarters in time to have breakfast on the terrace with GP. He has been reading while I've been out bird-watching.

'How was it HC?'

'Quite wonderful. I can't tell you all the names of the species we saw, but I felt the world was remade again. The birds make everything seem fresh, as it was when creation was young. Or something like that.'

'I'm so pleased the birds have returned to make their homes here. There will be challenges in the future. We will need to keep sticking up for them, as the Friend on the Bench did. And I'm pleased for you—I know this is important for you. But back to work. Now I want to start a new topic. Perhaps it seems strange to discuss this here in such a beautiful tranquil place. But so many people these days complain of stress, or even worse—burnout. I was reading a story from the UK about the CEO of a major bank, Antonio Horta-Osorio of Lloyds.'

'Yes, I think I remember. Who was Horta-Osorio?'

'Horta-Osorio was the ultimate business school high-flyer: he graduated in 1991 from INSEAD. Apparently, he was awarded the Henry Ford II Prize for the best student in that year. He also attended a six-week Advanced Management Program at Harvard Business School.'

'Hmmm. Should I be impressed?'

'So this is the story. He'd become so worried and anxious, around the time of the European sovereign debt crisis in 2011, apparently, that he'd lost the ability to sleep and had to stop work completely for six weeks. The Evening Standard called it the 'most high-profile sick leave in the City'.

'People talk of work-life balance, how it has become out of kilter, of working longer and longer hours, and how this makes people unhappy and ill. What do we make of this phenomenon, HC?'

'You're right, people do talk about it. I'm not sure I fully understand it. You must have had some experience of it, with employees perhaps.'

GP remains silent for a minute or two. 'Yes, there's certainly much talk of the work-life balance being skewed.

But maybe there's not much thinking about what this phrase work-life balance means.'

'Explain.'

## Are work and life separate?

'I mean that the phrase seems to imply a separation: you can put work in this compartment, and life in that one. Is that how things really are?'

'Well, that at least is how most people probably see it. They regard work as something they have to do out of necessity and look to fulfil themselves in the life outside work.'

'But is work separate from life? Surely it is very much part of life and in fact life itself. You have problems at home in the morning and you go to the office by 9 AM; but you are the same person. Your state of mind cannot be divided between home and office.

'So what I'm suggesting is this: Could it be this division between work and life which has bred all the confusion in the world of business—so many of the disasters and scandals we are always hearing about?'

Suddenly there's a diversion. I realize GP has put some kind of Bluetooth speaker on the table, and it begins to vibrate. 'Is it possible,' asks the voice of Panna, 'in daily life to live in a state which does not let this division come into being?'

I give GP a quizzical look. 'So how did you fix this up, GP?'

GP puts his finger to his lips. 'Just a simple piece of tech HC. Let Panna continue.'

'Or can we in our daily life establish the natural order of priority—health, family and work? '

'How do we understand this, Panna?' I ask.

'You need to understand the relationship that exists between you and your body, you and your family, you and your job. It is obvious that health is the first and most important thing. Without good health one cannot do anything worthwhile in life. Immediately after health the relationship with family comes into picture. Without an orderly and right relationship with family how do you expect to function well in your office? This natural order is obvious and not a prescription, nor is it being forced upon anybody.'

GP responds: 'I see this natural order quite clearly. It is sad how so many executives do tend to ignore the value of relations with their bodies and families. For them their work is everything: they worship work at the cost of their health and family relations. In fact

I heard that when asked why he wanted a biography written about him, Steve Jobs seems to have said a biography was required so that his children would know him better. This feels like a tragedy.'

There is a pause. There is a slight click from the speaker and it seems Panna has left us. We're sitting finishing our breakfast, a croissant, coffee, some fruit in my case. The birdsong is not as loud as earlier but still there is occasional chatter and movement. The world with all its strife and trouble and stress seems far away.

Eventually I break the silence. 'Panna's first question was, can we live in such a way that the division between life and work does not come into being? For many that seems to be impossible. So many people find their work repetitive and not meaningful, for a start. And others might say in their work they're forced to operate under pressures and incentives they would never bring into their home life.'

GP looks slightly stern for a moment. 'You know, HC, when addressing any complex issue, this approach may be useful: start with the whole, before getting lost in the details. Is it possible to look at life as a whole, and work as a whole? What do we mean by work, for a start, HC?'

'As I said, GP, most people seem to regard work as earning a living, a means to an end I suppose. Nose to the grindstone, the daily grind, and so on.'

'But do you regard work in that way?'

'No, but I'm hardly typical. I'm a writer after all. Many people don't consider what I do to be work at all. Maybe I went too far in the other direction, seeing work—in which I found my meaning—as the be-all and end-all of life.'

'Say more.'

'So many people view work as a kind of slavery. Wage slavery, they used to call it. People become deadened by the routine, going in to work day after day for forty years, used up, warped and worn out by it. That's a reality. But I wonder, is it also possible to become aware of all that, so that one either transforms one's work or leaves it.'

'Or the saying that if you do what you love doing, truly and with your full heart and humanity, you don't need to work even a day. So what I do is not separate from me.'

'Exactly, and what you do constitutes your calling, your raison d'être.'

## Suitability to the work

There's another pause. We get up from the breakfast table to stroll around the garden which surrounds the guest quarters.

'Would you agree that one of the fundamental things,' GP resumes, 'is understanding what work you are suited to, or called to? Certainly not everyone is called to be a writer. And not everyone is called to be a manager either. If your mind has a rural, farmerly bent, you are probably not cut out to be a stockbroker. So many people are forced into occupations they're not really suited to. If you are not suited to your work, if you are a square peg in a round hole, you will never feel that freedom we are talking about. The point is to understand the various influences the mind is filled with and how they operate in daily living.'

'So once again—you are saying—this is about understanding yourself, understanding the operations of the mind.'

## Effort and striving

'One of the common confusions, I would say,' continues GP, 'concerns effort and striving. People assume that if they put in more effort and strive harder, they will succeed. We see this in the phenomenon of longer and longer hours, especially in the US. Perhaps this was the case with the unfortunate banker.'

'The tree is made up of the roots, the trunk, the branches, the big ones and the little ones and the very delicate one that goes up there; and the leaf, the dead leaf, the withered leaf and the green leaf, the leaf that is eaten, the leaf that is ugly, the leaf that is dropping, the fruit, the flower—all that you see as a whole when you see the tree.'

*- Friend on the Bench*[1]

'Are you saying people shouldn't put in effort, shouldn't strive?'

'No, I'm just asking what all this effort and striving consists of. Can we ask whether it's possible to carry out the work in pressure cooker situations with a touch of lightness? Effort is both physical and psychological.

If your baby cries in the night, you won't find it an effort to comfort him or her, because you love your child. On the contrary if a neighbour disturbs you with noise during the night, your reaction will be different. Ultimately it boils down to whether one is doing what one loves. It comes down to how the mind responds to the work one does.'

'Sometimes writing—although I love my profession—feels like very hard work. One tries so hard to find the right words to convey what one is trying to say.'

'I'm no writer,' replies GP, 'but is that when you produce your best writing, when you are trying so hard?'

'No, probably not. It is more when you rather mysteriously ease up, when there's a flow.'

'Effort seems to be a desire to change things, not to stay with what is. When you stay with what is, without trying to change it, then you may find the problems have resolved themselves.'

## Coffee darshan—a pause in the day

It's mid-morning. The sun is now quite high in the sky, which is a deep pure blue, a colour you rarely see in polluted city air. Against the deep blue the red weathered rocks, sculpted into strange shapes, stand out and glow, almost as if they are on fire. GP comes up with a suggestion. 'Time for a break, HC?'

'Sure. Do you have something in mind?'

'I think you and I love a coffee break. Or you could say a coffee darshan.'

'You had better explain what darshan means.'

'I'll do that, but there's somewhere I want to take you to. A perfect place for coffee darshan, in fact.'

'Effort is distraction from what is. In the acceptance of what is, striving ceases. There is no acceptance when there is the desire to transform or modify what is. Striving, an indication of distraction, must exist so long as there is a desire to change what is.'

*– Friend on the Bench*[2]

'That sounds intriguing.'

'Well I think you'll find it is.'

We head to the car with me none the wiser where we're heading. As we drive out of the campus, a familiar voice speaks from the dashboard of the car.

'You're making a good decision. Many farmers I knew would never take a break. They thought the harder they worked the more money they would make, the more success they would have. But I observed my animals. Were they always 'working' as if on a treadmill? No, they knew when to take a break. Sometimes the cows will just lie down and ruminate. The effort you were talking of is either in the physical domain or psychological domain. The real problem of effort is in the psychological domain and not in the physical domain. If someone tells you to lift iron slabs of 100kgs you will not be able to do it because you just cannot lift the slabs. In that sense there is no problem whatsoever in the physical domain. But to do a simple thing like getting up early and going to the office on Monday morning, you find you may moan and groan. This pain you experience is more in the psychological domain. Nothing physical about it.'

Panna's voice fades away. We are driving towards the local town, which GP tells me used to be a sleepy place, but is experiencing a boom, and expanding beyond its old limits. We stop on the outskirts, in what seems to be a green oasis. Here there is a rather special café.

The café, named Café Darshan, is designed as an elegant long hut, made of natural materials, bamboo and thatch, which sits unobtrusively among the trees and flowering shrubs. There are tables both outside and inside. The atmosphere is calm and meditative, not bustling.

'I thought you'd like this place, HC', GP says as we order coffee and croissants from a middle-aged woman wearing a sari, whose smile of welcome is unforced and free of the strain which often afflicts people working in hospitality. She and GP obviously know each other.

'This is my friend HC,' says GP by way of introduction. 'He lives in England but was born here and studied at the School in the Valley as a child.'

'I also studied at the School in the Valley,' replies the woman. 'I moved to the big city to work, then my husband and I decided to return here, to start something a little different. We wanted to source everything as locally as possible, especially the coffee, which comes from a neighbouring state; to work with local coffee farmers, to be part of the whole process of production. It's possible to grow coffee, we believe, in a way that doesn't damage nature, without using pesticides.' She smiles again.

'That seems rather encouraging,' I offer. 'I can't wait for the coffee. But can you explain the name of your Café? Why Café Darshan?'

## A Meeting by the River

'We're not using this word in a very technical sense, as a Hindu philosopher might,' the woman explains. Christopher Isherwood has defined 'Darshan' beautifully in his book 'A Meeting by the River'—maybe you know it. Darshan means exposing oneself to the vibrations of a holy man or a deity. This is the traditional sense of it. But what we are trying to do by calling our place Café Darshan is to encourage people to take a break, take a pause, look inward not outward—and share whatever comes up with the friend who may be with them.'

'You may think you have but actually you have no relationship when the whole of your mind is occupied with one's own progress, with one's anxieties, with one's own problems and so on. It is so obvious. But though it is very obvious we do nothing about it. On the contrary, we work at it, improve it—it is called self-improvement, to become better, but always within the narrow limits.'

*- Friend on the Bench*[3]

'I think I understand,' exclaims GP, suddenly very animated. 'You mean to look inward into all the fallacies or illusions that one's own mind has created for itself. Let us say there is a possibility to have Darshan of one's own latest goof-ups. This can help one to see the inner workings of a situation and see things as they are, without pressure or compulsion—not to exercise conscious choice, skip uncomfortable things, but face and be with whatever comes up.'

The woman smiles again. 'Yes, you could say that.'

I hadn't noticed but GP has brought the small Bluetooth speaker into the café. Panna seems to know where we are. 'Do you know one of the essential features of good management is not to goof up in delivering a service to a customer? How to prevent a goof up seems to be the name of the game. Much like this, a pause in the day in the name of coffee darshan may enable one to see the fallacies inside oneself and go beyond.'

'I agree with Panna,' responds GP. 'I firmly believe this pause in the day can help with getting through the daily grind of work and alleviating the heavy burden. It may even bring a touch of lightness. One can open up to a friend, as you and I might do. Some executives may simply consider it a waste of time though in reality it is the time to refresh oneself. It won't necessarily provide a solution but as one opens up one exposes problems to oneself. One can try it out.'

'And a café can often be the right place?'

'So long as the coffee is right, the place is right. A certain peacefulness and quietness are important.

There's a pause and I take in not just the ambience but the beautiful smell of roasted coffee beans. When our coffee arrives it seems to have a special aroma—one almost senses the greenness of forest leaves together with suggestions of roasted nuts and chocolate.

'Nobody can live in isolation. To live is to be related. It is only in the mirror of relationship that I understand myself, which means that I must be extraordinarily alert in my thoughts, feelings, and actions in relationship.'

*– Friend on the Bench*[4]

GP seems to be reading my mind. 'Just the feel of the aroma of coffee as you enter the coffee shop. This feel means a lot in everything you do.'

'Savouring the taste, the smell…'

'But also reflecting on those who have grown the crop, the seasonal variation, the nuances in the process of coffee production, tending to the plants, picking, drying and roasting the beans. And the attention paid by the barista to the making of the coffee in the café.'

'Maybe that quality of attention can percolate through into how we live the rest of the day.'

'This is not the way everyone thinks about a coffee break.'

'You may know there are also coffee shops, some branded ones originating from the US where you hardly get the smell of the coffee even if you resort to some breathing techniques. A so-called coffee break could mean, for example for an executive working in Silicon Valley, driving in the car with the paper cup of a well-known brand of coffee in the cup-holder by the side of the seat, with the mind in a tangle of thoughts about the day ahead, which could be mixed up with what went on at home that morning.'

'But that is not really paying attention to the joy of drinking coffee, or indeed to the office work itself: that is not coffee darshan. That is not living in the moment.'

'No. You are neither enjoying coffee nor are you doing any office work not to speak of appreciating the beautiful scenery you can see around you while driving the car.'

'We are using coffee as an illustration. One may take something else. It may be a glass of juice. Or tea. Or just a glass of water. What's important is to have that pause in the day just to reflect or sit quietly. We have invented anti-virus software which scans the computer for any viruses. But shouldn't we have an equivalent 'software', or just awareness, when it comes to seeing through the viruses that are operating within?'

We sit for a while in the peaceful place, taking in what's been said. There is no rush to return to the School so we order one more coffee. At least I order one more coffee. I find the aroma and taste quite irresistible. GP is content with water.

## Relationship

I am sipping my coffee. GP has a thought. 'There is one basic fact that we haven't drawn enough attention to. Everything must surely be understood in terms of relationship. There is no life outside relationship.'

'I agree, but what do we mean by relationship?'

'Can we agree that generally speaking by relationship one understands the relationship between a man and woman or boy and girl? Or we may take it to mean family relationships like the ones we have with mother or father or sister or brother or man and man, woman and woman and so on?'

'Agreed.'

'But in reality relationship exists with everything around you. You have relationship with property, with ideas, with your background, with nature. By relationship we mean response of the mind. If the mind does not respond to a certain thing in life it may mean there is no relationship. In the mirror of relationship one can see oneself as one truly is.'

'Say more.'

'For instance, suddenly while walking on a street you see someone drop a hundred dollar bill: what is your response? If you are able to observe the response of your mind, it is possible for you to understand what kind of a person you are.'

## To live is to be related

'The understanding of oneself does not come through the process of withdrawal from society or through retirement into an ivory tower. If you and I really go into the matter carefully and intelligently, we will see that we can understand ourselves only in relationship and not in isolation.'

– *Friend on the Bench*[5]

'If I do not understand myself, the whole of relationship is one of confusion in ever-widening circles. So, relationship becomes of extraordinary importance, not with the so-called mass, the crowd, but in the world of my family and friends, however small that may be—my relationship with my wife, my children, my neighbour.'

'Life is a movement in relationship.'

– *Friend on the Bench*[6]

The Bluetooth speaker begins to vibrate. 'The same goes, GP,' comments Panna, 'for your relationship with the job you are doing every day for your livelihood. If you are CEO of a company—as you have been, GP—are you treating that position as a function or as a kind of status symbol? Here you have to be alert to see if the relationship is spilling over into the psychological realm instead of remaining in the physical realm. This spilling over is a surefire formula for disorder. You may test this out. As a CEO if you think you are superior to your team members your ability to extract the best out of them is doubtful.'

'You are right, Panna. You are saying that the difference is only in function and not at a human level.'

'Of course. At a human level all human beings are at the same level. A cook and a Prime Minister, the President and his driver, are the same at the human level; the difference is only in function. This relationship exists all through life with something or other. Life itself is movement in relationship. The world or the society is the network of relationships you have with everything in life.

'If you go to a mango orchard and eat a delicious mango obviously you will enjoy it. But if you are able to relate to the state of the mind of the farmer your appreciation of the eating experience is at a different level.'

'And the same goes for coffee,' I put in.

'If we do not understand relationship our actions also may produce not only confusion; they may even result in conflict.

'And by the way the understanding of oneself—which is the most important part of core of management—is not something superhuman. There are two major tools, if we can call them that, as I believe we have discussed before, that are greatly helpful in understanding the workings of the mind: we can refer to them as the mirror of relationship and negation. Please don't mistake the tool of negation and mirror of relationship as techniques

'Action has meaning only in relationship. Without understanding relationship, action on any level will only bring conflict. The understanding of relationships is infinitely more important than the search for any plan of action.'

*– Friend on the Bench*[7]

which can be learned and applied. These are human spontaneous processes.

'As in the case of rivers you may not easily see the source of the waters but what you see is how the waters gather momentum as they move and deepen. If you go into this process patiently with care, you will see how it begins to gather momentum.'

There is a slight click from the speaker: it seems that Panna has finished. GP continues: 'Another dimension of relationship to be aware of is this: you may think you have relationship with another but actually you have no relationship with another if the whole of your mind is occupied with your own progress, with your own anxieties, with your own problems and so on.'

'That is so true, GP. I suppose we've all been guilty of that.'

'So if you are talking of work-life balance it is important to establish a right relationship with everything around you. Let us assume the job you do is mostly for livelihood. You need to be aware why you are doing whatever you are doing. Health is the most important part of life. What is your relationship with your body? Are you so obsessed with it that you need to develop a six pack by going to the gym?'

'Not in my case!'

'Alternatively your attitude can be to treat your body with responsibility, in order to keep it fit and healthy. For example, many knee problems can be treated by strengthening five muscles—calf, quadra, ham, adductor, abductor. Essentially it is a human body. So it deserves to be treated as such.'

'And your body is not separate from you. You are your body. And once you see that, maybe you are less likely to abuse it, do violence to it.'

'Good point, HC! Then comes the relationship with one's family: without this being in a good place how do you expect to perform

## Relationship with desire

'The question is "Is it wrong to have desires and passions?" The first thing to see is that any form of condemnation puts an end to every thought or thinking, to every form of investigation and enquiry. A mind which functions in `do's' and 'don'ts,' is the most stupid mind. Unfortunately, most of us are educated with stupidity; when we can get over that, we can begin to enquire into the whole problem of desire, not if it is right or wrong but to understand it. Because, if we understand something, then it is no longer a problem to us.'

— *Friend on the Bench*[8]

well in your job? This is so obvious. Right relationship first with health, then with family and then with the work. Without good health how do you maintain good relations with your family and without these two being in good order how can you do your best in your job? Health, Family and Work–this is the right and natural order. This is not a prescription, by the way!'

## Status and function

'A common confusion has to do with function and status,' GP resumes.

'I'm not sure I follow.'

'People confuse function and status. Functionally speaking a car is a merely practical means of getting about. Then it becomes a status symbol. When the mind moves this relationship with the car from the functional domain—which is a physical domain—into the psychological domain the disorder starts. This sounds simple but is actually rather profound. You may dispute this HC, as a wine connoisseur, but I'm convinced some people drink certain fine wines, not because they really enjoy the smell and taste of that wine, but because they think it is a sign of status to be seen drinking it.'

'Certainly true of some,' I agree. 'And the same goes for art collectors. Some truly love the works they collect. Others employ so-called experts to collect for them. Big names, and so on. The price tag must be fixed very visibly on the artwork.'

'And this relates to the wider question of fame. Fame has nothing to do with function. Just being famous doesn't make you a good manager or entrepreneur, or anything else, come to that. If you follow the illusion of fame you become an illusion yourself.'

'That's true of writers also,' I muse.

## Life as a whole

'We've talked about work as a whole. But as we've said work and life can't really be separated. So we have to look at life as a whole.' GP turns towards me, almost as if throwing down a challenge.

'That seems so daunting, so many problems, so many issues…'

'Yes, the tendency is to break it down into all these different problems, work problems, relationship problems, health problems, money problems. But are they all separate?'

'No, probably not. If I have a problem with my wife or husband it may prove to be not unconnected to the problem I have with my boss or manager.'

'And if you try to solve all those problems separately, it only leads to greater confusion, because they are all related to something more fundamental.'

'But how can we solve all those problems simultaneously? That's surely too much for any human being.'

## Money, sex and fame?

GP smiles. 'I think there is a way and we will come to it. But in the meantime, can we together consider three areas which cause maximum confusion and disorder in life—money, sex and fame. Most of the disorders in life seem to arise out of the distorted relationship with these three things. These seem to be preoccupations of many businessmen and women and to lead them astray. We're familiar, I think, with some of these stories—we've talked about them before.'

'I think I have one I can tell you, but why don't you start?'

'All right, I'll begin with the story of Jho Low: the subtitle could be, how much money and fame are enough?

'Jho Low is a Malaysian financier, currently wanted by the US Justice Department on charges of fraud and on the run from

'If I know how to run the motor, the engine, it is no problem to me; I do not say it is wrong or right, I know how to work it. If I do not know, I do not condemn the motor. The same is the case with desires. It is no use getting confused or frightened encouraging or condemning them. If I can understand the workings of desire, then the desire is no problem. It is only the fearful attitude towards desire, that creates the problem.'

*– Friend on the Bench*[9]

police. He comes from a wealthy family and was educated at the famous English public school Harrow (where Winston Churchill and Jawaharlal Nehru were also schooled). I believe George Bernard Shaw wrote somewhere: 'Education does not make a man good. It only makes him clever, mostly for mischief'.'

'That was certainly true of some of the people I came across from those schools, when I was at university in England and afterwards.'

'But it seems this wealth and privilege were not enough for Low. He came to prominence in the 2010s partly as a result of A-list connections and an extremely lavish lifestyle, including the giving of gifts to celebrities, purchase of a superyacht and private jet, and also of paintings by Monet and Picasso. He was involved in the financing of the Hollywood movie The Wolf of Wall Street through a production company called Red Granite. He gave parties that were extravagant even by celebrity standards and became known as the 'Asian Great Gatsby'. Rotund and bespectacled, he appeared a rather shy character, happier to observe the antics of his celebrity friends than to participate.'

'I've come across one or two others like that.'

'Then questions began to be asked about the source of the apparently unlimited money. These led to investigations which revealed a massive fraud: the money Low spent had apparently been siphoned from a Malaysian Sovereign Wealth Fund called 1MDB, set up supposedly to benefit the Malaysian people but in practice acting as a conduit to enrich a coterie of officials and businessmen including the ex-Prime Minister of Malaysia, Najib Razak and Low himself. Some of the details were truly astonishing: $250 million was spent on a superyacht, $35 million on a private jet and $200 million on artwork.'

'A fascinating story. So here is my tale. It concerns the British politician John Profumo, and it could be subtitled: why do we pursue sex at all costs? You may ask, why Profumo? He was a politician and not a manager. Well, I would answer that he is a human being in the first place. Even a manager is a human being in the first place. All human beings have the same vulnerabilities.

'So Profumo served as Secretary of State for War in the cabinet of the Conservative Prime Minister Harold Macmillan. Profumo met a 19-year-old would-be model called Christine Keeler at a house party at Cliveden, the home of Lord Astor, in July 1961. They began an affair. Keeler was then living with the society osteopath Dr Stephen Ward. Ward was very well connected, through his practice, with high society circles and liked to give somewhat louche parties. Profumo sometimes met Keeler at Ward's house. Another acquaintance of Ward, and Profumo, was a Russian naval attaché, Captain Yevgeny Ivanov, with whom Keeler had also had a brief relationship.'

'Ah, I'm beginning to remember the story. Please continue.'

'So as rumours about these goings-on began to circulate, and as an unofficial investigation by the Labour MP George Wigg gathered evidence, Profumo made a statement to the House of Commons denying any impropriety in his relationship with Ms Keeler. But the rumours intensified and press reports hinting at the relationships between Profumo, Keeler and Ivanov appeared. Ward was investigated and then charged by the police for living off immoral earnings. Under this pressure, despite publicly backing Profumo, Ward indicated to Profumo's private secretary and to the Home Secretary that embarrassing revelations might emerge. The Prime Minister, who had previously supported Profumo, summoned him back to London from a holiday with his wife in Venice and Profumo admitted having lied to the House of Commons. He tendered his resignation. He never returned to politics but spent the rest of his working life in the charitable sector. In a recent BBC TV dramatization of the events, Profumo's rather laconic wife makes the comment 'I hope she was worth it'.'

'And I seem to recall that it did not end well for Ward. He committed suicide. A victim of the establishment, you might say. So what do these stories tell us?'

'It seems,' I say after a pause, 'that many of the things we pursue so avidly are will-o'-the-wisp or what Medieval writers called *ignes fatui*—delusions which lead us astray.

'One of them, obviously is pleasure—sex being the most extreme or addictive form of pleasure. Many people seem to confuse pleasure and happiness.'

'Explain further.'

'Pleasure is gratification of the senses, is it not? But the satisfaction from that quickly wanes and then it needs to be stimulated again. And so on, on an endless merry-go-round. Is that happiness?'

'Clearly not. But still happiness for many appears to be the most important aim. Even the American Declaration of Independence speaks of 'Life, Liberty and the Pursuit of Happiness."

'But if we were truly happy, would we be seeking happiness?'

'And so we have to ask what these things are really, what is money, what is sex, what is fame?'

'Or what they mean to us,' I offer. 'For Jho Low, perhaps, money, or very large sums of it, and fame made him something he was not—a person at the centre of things socially, a celebrity or friend of celebrities. Though one may well ask what is celebrity. And what about sex, which seems the driver in so many of these cases?'

'Yes, sex is often pursued at all costs, as in the case of Profumo, a man who apparently had everything, wealth, a successful career, a happy family life.'

'Why is that?' I ponder. 'Is it just for the transient pleasure or sensation? Then you are surely building on shaky foundations. Does the Friend on the Bench have much to say on this subject?'

'Oh yes; there's no aspect of life that escapes him, and this is one of the most universal of all subjects. What he has to say seems surprising at first: that the reason people are so obsessed by sex, prepared to sacrifice almost anything for it, has more to do with what surrounds sex than with sex itself. People are so hemmed in and restricted in their everyday lives, intellectually, emotionally and spiritually; sex seems to be the one area where there can be complete forgetfulness of self. In that moment, when he was with Christine, perhaps Profumo felt free of all the striving and effort, all the calculation and careerism.'

'Didn't he also say once that thought gives shape to sensations? Those sensations, once they have taken shape, continue as memory and create a kind of haunting ground in the mind. If we are not aware the mind will continue to be haunted by those things and there will be no end to it all.'

'So we're agreed on one thing at least. All this boils down to understanding the operations of the mind. Isn't that the answer?'

## Conclusion

'We're not at the end of the road, HC, but what do you think we've accomplished on this road trip of ours? Have we in fact got anywhere at all? Have we clarified something, anything? Are we closer to what we were searching for?'

I reflect for a moment before answering. 'We were trying, I believe, to get closer to the core of management—a bit closer perhaps than some of the schools and gurus have managed. We proceeded partly by the tool of negation—working out what management was not.

'Management is not anything technical, we decided. It is not really something that can be taught by any technical training. We compared the manager—or the entrepreneur, as we decided the two terms were to some extent interchangeable—to the conductor of an orchestra. The conductor doesn't play an instrument but guides the way the orchestra plays and the piece goes, sets the tempo and so on. The good conductor is an excellent listener, and can gauge the state of the players, tell if anything is amiss, and so on. The conductor has a feel—we will come back to that.

'We distinguished between two kinds of business: business-to-consumer, and business-to-business. They seem to require two very different mind-sets, one more merchant-like, the other more farmer-like. This distinction could be very important for a person trying to work out what is their calling.

'We worked out that management is not a thing, but a verb in the active present. We might do better to talk about managing than management.

'Throughout we have been guided by Panna, the farmer with the feel and the passion. Even though he is no longer with us, somehow he has found a way to communicate with us. Panna's farmerly approach involved listening to, being in tune with, the animals and crops he cared for. For him farming was a passion and a vocation, not a means of getting rich. This farmerly approach might be more appropriate for someone intending to work in the business-to-business sector rather than the business-to-consumer sector.

'Panna in turn was impacted by the Friend on the Bench, the founder of this school, and someone who has helped both you and me to gain some clarity in life. The Friend on the Bench cannot be categorized as one of the many educators in the ordinary sense of the word. What he spoke of covers the whole field of human existence. In that sense you could say he is the educator of life.'

'So far so good, but that doesn't sound like the core yet.'

'You're right. OK. So we also came to the conclusion that we cannot reach the core of management by looking at only external factors. This is where all the schools and gurus fall down. We need to look inwards, whilst not neglecting the external factors; after all, we need to be aware how our minds are responding to them. Then there is complete observation. Otherwise we are led by fragmented observation.'

'So we need to understand the mind.'

'Which isn't at all simple.'

'We compared the mind to a computer, didn't we? We discussed the hidden programming of the computer, not just software, which ordinary users can interact with, but the hidden operating systems which condition everything. They can't be accessed by the ordinary user but they affect all the operations of the computer. Perhaps the mind has similar operating systems, which we call conditioning. We discussed how we can become aware of and perhaps ultimately be free of this conditioning. We talked about computer viruses and how much attention is paid to them. The mind also seems to have its viruses but less attention is paid to them.'

'The computer is just memory and software and operating systems, isn't it? The mechanical mind is like that also.'

It seems Panna has one more contribution to make. The Bluetooth speaker is once again vibrating.

'There is something beyond the mechanical mind. There is something beyond conditioning. We human beings can become aware of our conditioning and of the operations of the mind. We can become aware of our own thinking, feeling, reacting, in the moment, moment by moment. Then we have a chance to watch ourselves, not to react. We can see, for example, that we are our anger, that it is not separate from us. The manager must start by observing his or her own mind.'

The rest of the day passes peacefully for both of us. An afternoon rest followed by our customary game of tennis, then supper once again at the Director's house.

# 11

# The Unique Feel of Roger Federer

## *A golden era in tennis watching*

---

GP and I will be staying a few more days at the School in the Valley. I'm keen to do more birdwatching and I've agreed to speak at the morning assembly about what it means to me to be a writer. How I'm happy to be a writer in different media, from journalism to poetry. Writing as a craft and also as a vocation. GP, for his part, has some meetings connected with the School's management and fundraising. It's also an opportunity to play another game or two of tennis. We join up in the late afternoon for a doubles with two younger players, one of them a coach.

After tennis, back at the guest quarters in the birdhaunted woods, we have a chance to talk about someone we both admire greatly. This is not an entrepreneur or writer on management but the tennis player Roger Federer.

'I know we both admire Federer—and maybe as more than just a tennis player,' I begin, 'but what does he have to do with management?'

GP pauses before responding. 'Well I think we can agree this has nothing with sports management, or anything connected with finance. We will not be talking here about how Mark McCormack and IMG took over the tennis world. For McCormack tennis players were 'pawns in the massive, changing, vigorously competitive arenas of advertising and marketing.' But that is not our interest.'

'Funnily enough the first piece I had ever published, in the Spectator magazine in London, was on that subject. I called it The Tennis Business. But carry on.'

'In my view Roger Federer has transformed the art of tennis watching. Federer has brought a whole new phalanx of viewers to tennis, who are attracted not for nationalistic or chauvinistic reasons, or even just because of success and winning, but because of the relationship with the beauty that is manifested in his game. This cuts across all ages, nationalities and religions. Federer has transformed the relationship of viewers to the game. Until he came on the scene most of the time, for most people, it was just watching a sport, but with Federer playing, for spectators all over the world it became watching not just sport, but sharing the experience of beauty and art. With this he brought many new viewers to tennis.

'We also need to define the relationship that spectators have with watching tennis. We should be under no illusion that all spectators are there to appreciate the beauty of the game. There could be spectators who are watching because their countryman is playing. If this is the case they don't care how he wins as long as he wins. The relationship with the game is more or less non-existent, as it appears to be the patriotism that draws them to watch the match. There could be teams of analysts watching to analyse the strengths and weaknesses of players as the next round opponent is the player they are working for. Their relation is only as analysts. Other than competitive tennis players, there are also many tennis players at club level in many towns and cities across the world. There are players who play for the joy of playing the game. This is also a great way of keeping fit and healthy, both in mind and body. Unfortunately there are quite a few pretenders of the game where egos spill over into the tennis court and spoil the atmosphere of many a tennis club in the world.'

'I agree with you, GP—including about the pretenders. We have some of those at my club. First of all, though, I guess we should try to focus on what makes Federer's game special, before we draw out the wider conclusions. You mention artistic beauty, the aesthetic side. Personally I've never seen a player with a game as beautiful, as aesthetically satisfying, as Federer's. The word artistic is important, I think. I recall his fitness coach Pierre Paganini saying that essentially Federer is an artist, who also plays tennis, and that makes him different from pretty much all other players.'

'You're a writer, HC. You presumably think about aesthetic matters quite a bit. What are we talking about when we say he's an artist?'

I pause. 'Well, we could apply the tool of negation. Federer is not someone who biffs and bashes the ball relentlessly—a baseline grinder. I remember him saying he couldn't bear to play like that. He's quite the opposite of that.'

'We could say there are two categories of tennis players. Those who belong to class G and those who belong to class B.'

'What are these classes, GP ?'

'G is Grinders, the class most tennis players belong to. They believe in percentage tennis—just keep putting the ball into the opponents' court and hope for a mistake by the opponent. It is a bore to watch these players even though they may be champions of multiple grand slams. It is literally a pain in the neck if you are sitting on the side galleries of the court. It may be tolerable for someone watching the game for nationalistic reasons, to put up with the pain in the neck.'

'And B?'

'B is beautiful. Until Federer came on the scene we did not see any one playing tennis with such beauty or grace, on a sustained basis for such a long period, nor did we know such a possibility existed. B class is a new category invented by Federer. This is a paradigm shift in the evolution of Tennis. Even Federer's great rival Rafael Nadal has acknowledged this.'

'I agree entirely. For me artistry, which is connected to beauty, has to do with improvisation, the unexpected, a childlike joy and wonderment, as well as beauty. All this is connected to the feel, which we will come back to.'

'So many times, we see Federer produce a jawdropping shot, a shot no-one else could have thought of, let alone executed.

'I remember him playing Andy Murray in the final at Wimbledon one year—2012 I think—and Murray had won the first set and was dominating. Suddenly, out of the blue, Federer produced two exquisite drop volleys to break Murray's serve at 5-6 in the second set. That turned the whole match around. It was improvisation, imagination, grace, not grinding power.'

'And this is what draws in the spectators, makes them feel they are watching beauty in action, as if they were at the ballet, rather than two grinders going through a hard day at the office. Funnily enough that's a phrase the commentators often use.'

We continue our discussion. 'Federer has often spoken about his joy in the game, which also extends to watching a lot of tennis himself. He watches women's tennis, men's tennis, he knows all the players, he does this for pure enjoyment. I believe Federer has often said that he plays tennis—and continued as a professional far longer than nearly all his peers—simply because he loves playing. Of course he is almost uniquely gifted, has been incredibly successful and has been handsomely rewarded. But those are not the reasons he has continued playing. You could see it in the way he plays—with a sense of fun and creativity, sometimes even cheekiness.'

'There's something else we need to say about watching, HC. It's about the way Federer watches the ball.'

'Well yes. I think I've told you before how I once saw a slow-motion replay of Federer hitting a backhand. He seemed to keep watching even after the ball had left the racket. But I believe this is quite a deep subject. We will return to it.'

I pause again. 'So how does all this relate to the themes of our little book on management?'

'I remember that early on we made a distinction between technical and non-technical work. How the work of the manager is non-technical. Here I think we are not talking about anything technical. I expect whole books have been written about Federer's forehand grip, or his beautiful one-handed backhand. But we are not discussing anything like that. Ultimately, we are talking about understanding the operations of the mind. Federer has said that the mental side of winning a grand slam tournament, to stay focused and healthy through so many matches, is the toughest.'

'Yes,' I interrupt. 'He's never been one for special diets, like some other players I might mention, has he?'

'Exactly. He has always looked after his body but he has done so in a more relaxed way than other players. I've heard him say he enjoys chocolate and wine. 'I like to eat a bit of everything. I'm a healthy person. I like to have my desserts from time to time. I like to have a glass of wine or a glass of champagne. I like my pastas before the game.' By the way, it became a habit for me to watch a Federer match and then go on to read the press interview he did afterwards. These interviews are almost as impressive and interesting as his performances on the court! They have helped me to feel the depth of the game and relate to the state of mind of Federer. In one of the interviews Federer said, 'Of course I would be happy if I could equal such a significant record,' then added 'but I'm not planning to chase the most titles. The priority is health and family. Everything else is secondary."

'But of course, it's not just his body that he looks after. He takes care of his mental wellbeing above all.'

'Yes, he prioritizes family relationships, first with his parents (who have attended most of his matches), then with his wife Mirka and two pairs of twins; he has not played too many tournaments. He likes to take time off, he's said, to go to the city, to read the paper—in the spirit of the coffee darshan we talked about. So he's a perfect example of the so-called work-life balance we were talking about. In fact his is a classic case of work-life balance as the natural order of health, family and work is so wonderfully maintained. This is a great example for managers who go through pressure cooker situations in their work.'

I reflect further. 'Also relevant to our view of management, I feel, is Federer's sceptical opinion of role-models, coaches and pundits. Federer admires certain players (Edberg, Sampras) but never talks about modelling his game on anyone else's. He has employed coaches, but usually with less hype and more modesty and in a more light-hearted way than certain other players. 'It's important to listen to people you trust,' he has said. 'But to listen to everybody is not the right thing either."

'Yes, Peter Lundgren was his coach at one time. Lundgren also coached Marcelo Rios who had achieved a No.1 ranking without ever winning a Grand Slam tournament. But Lundgren said Rios needed a psychologist not a coach. What is a coach if not a psychologist? So I think Roger was right to move on from Lundgren. Psychologically he has a role to play. But I doubt technically he can do much except suggest a few tweaks or study the game of the opponents and offer suggestions to his ward.'

'He has also spent time without a coach. Ljubicic certainly seemed to play a useful role. Nadal used his cross court top spin forehand very effectively to Federer's backhand most of the time. Federer's association with Ljubicic coincided with the time when Roger started to hit his backhand topspin on the rise, against Nadal. This could be described as a tweak in the technique but it took time off Nadal and effectively reduced Nadal's strength. With this tweak in his approach Roger went on to defeat Nadal six times out of seven, starting with the Australian Open in 2017. But Ljubicic is as much a friend as a coach.'

'We talked about Federer's 'feel'. How would you define that?'

'We can start by using the tool of negation, as we have frequently done before. What is Federer's 'feel' not?'

'Well, it has very little to do with coaching, for a start, as we've said. His 'feel' is not something he learned in an academy. You almost certainly couldn't teach it.'

'So it might be comparable to the 'feel' Panna had for his animals, or the conductor Karajan had for his players.'

'When he is at his best, there is a unique flow to his game. It is graceful and seamless, and almost never brutal; it is about being in the moment, rather than following some prearranged game plan.'

'The feel is mental as much as physical. Or more mental than physical.'

## Most Compassionate shot

GP pauses again, then chuckles. 'I consider his tweener winner against his opponent Djokovic in the 2009 US Open semi-final to be the most compassionate winner in the history of tennis—he was able to pass his opponent while looking in the opposite direction.'

'Why do you call this a compassionate shot, GP? '

'Based on my understanding from my exposure to the Friend on the Bench let me explain this. The point was won by Federer not by any brutal hitting or wicked slicing. You know too well how the game is played today. It is essentially won by brutal hitting or outhitting the opponent. Whereas in this shot no brutal hitting is involved. It is a completely nonviolent shot. Compassion in the first place has its own action and certainly not based on will. Since it has its own action it is the seeing and the playing at the same time. Whether Federer is with his back to the net or seeing or not seeing where the net is and where the opponent is or is not on the other side—none of this matters. Because it is his mind's eye that is seeing. I am told a mind's eye is much, much more capable. In that state the player is the court, the player is the racket, the player is the tennis ball. There is no separation whatsoever. There is no such thing as the watcher, nor the watched. Only a state of watching remains. This is a pure transcendental moment. In fact, the opponent should feel blessed in that moment because he is one of the causes of that shot and a closest witness.'

'I'm not sure Djokovic saw it that way but carry on.'

'From Federer's angle the challenge is to remain in that state of compassion which he seems to have experienced in that moment. It is not about naming that moment; that is just words. Remaining in that moment is the essence. It is not dependent on any result nor does it seek any result. The result is obvious and purely depends on the technical abilities. Federer's technical abilities are never in question. Maybe Federer is the only player in the history of tennis to remain in that moment. You could see it as pure energy operating in an absolute state which is neither capable of being hurt nor capable of hurting anyone. Can this be called the 'celestial quality' where the subtle body combines with the subtle mind? This celestial beauty is absolute and certainly beyond measure. It is an absolute state uncontaminated by thought. You know how we mess up a shot when we think too much about the shot. The state of mind of Federer at that moment is not something one can seek. It should happen naturally. It is a moment of magic you can say. Compassion is that state where one has the mind that is not capable of being hurt nor does it hurt anyone. For instance in this case the opponent cannot complain or regret his inability to win the point. He simply learns to live with this moment. Other players who have come to know of this shot may also try to seek this moment, but their effort may last a lifetime and yet that moment may not arrive.'

'But there's a difference. Only Federer is such a natural human being, that he could be in contact with that pure energy in that moment. As his fitness coach Pierre Paganini once said, 'it's particularly important that the man he is embodies the player he is."

'He may not even recollect that exact state of that moment because the brain might not have recorded the quality of that moment. This not-recording the moment is another natural quality of that energy as it would have recorded only the functional side of that shot. Federer surely remembers that shot. But I don't think even Federer can recapitulate the state of mind when that shot was played. Even if he does recapitulate it that is only description and that description is not the described. Nor can he recognize that moment in the future. If he does recognize it that could amount to going into the past to compare and that is not living in the moment in its entirety. Federer—or anyone else—can see that recorded shot on YouTube by simply searching for 'tweener 2009 US SF'. But I doubt he can recapture that moment of his state of mind as that moment has come and gone like a great moment of joy.'

'This is also what we are talking of in this book, is it not, GP? The essence is not the technical but the non-technical qualities of the manager. I'm not sure we can stretch this as far as that shot of Federer. But at least the feel we are talking of is in that direction. One should look for that direction in management.

'In fact,' I continue, 'Federer has consistently shown compassion towards other players, especially those he has beaten rather easily.

This occurred with Philipp Kohlschreiber at the Monte Carlo Open in 2011 after a match which Federer won in less than an hour. A journalist was congratulating Federer on his easy win saying– 'in less than an hour a nice work out, 50 minutes?'—and Federer said, 'Don't be too harsh on Philipp. Look, he also tried his best.'

'I would say Federer has also shown compassion towards his watchers, as when he continued to play in the 2008 Wimbledon against Nadal in the fading light. He didn't think it would be right to make the spectators come back next day, or miss the end of the match. He said in an interview, 'I kept on playing. It would have been brutal for fans, media, for us, for everybody, to come back tomorrow. But what are you going to do? It's rough on me obviously to lose maybe the biggest tournament in the world over maybe a bit of light, you know'.'

I sit for a moment recalling that extraordinary final. How Federer came back from two sets down against a rampaging Nadal—above all in the fourth set tie-break, when Federer saved a match point with what I consider the greatest backhand passing shot of all time, struck with supreme grace under the most extreme pressure. By the end of the match, I felt it had transcended winning and losing.

'What do you think about the famous GOAT debate, GP? Who is or was the greatest tennis player of all time? Federer, or Nadal or Djokovic? Or someone else?'

'The decision on the GOAT, in my view, cannot be purely based on the number of Grand Slam titles. It has to take into account the player's wider impact on the world of tennis and the qualitative aspects of his game.

'Roger is the GOAT. This is not a matter of debate or argument. Let us examine this more deeply—first the whole, then the details. To decide this question you need to observe the whole of the tennis world. We can take a clock face as an image of this. Let us map the world of tennis on the face of an analogue clock. The greatness needs to be spread across the whole area of the circle. The whole of the tennis world consists first of the player's box where his coach, physio, manager, family and friends normally sit. Beyond this little gang in the player's box, there is a far greater army of many divisions consisting of organizers, ball kids, officials, umpires, statisticians, manufacturers of tennis gear, tennis analysts, journalists of print media and digital media, sponsors and advertisers (in stadia, on dress, shoes, rackets, bill boards etc.) and finally by far the largest division, spectators—in the stadium and outside the stadium like Henman Hill and the hundreds of millions of TV viewers spread across the world.

'Surely a player's greatness is not measured just by winning accolades in the little world of the player's box which, on the clock face, could take the space of just a minute or two or generously speaking, maybe five minutes. Five minutes take up about 8.33 percentage of the clock face. If you look at the wider world of tennis, the vast majority of the area is occupied by the mass of the entities other than player's box.'

I can see GP is getting quite carried away by this. I decide to introduce another element. 'How about betting, GP? That's quite big business and we haven't mentioned it.'

GP frowns. 'I have not added it in the list above as unfortunately betting is a tainted thing. But do you know the story of Nick Newlife?'

'No, but I like the name.'

'The name turns out to be somewhat ironic. In 2003 Mr Newlife placed a bet of £1520 on Federer winning seven Wimbledon titles. By the time Federer won his seventh title in 2012 Nick Newlife, despite his name, was no longer alive. But this gentleman had stipulated in his will that any winnings from his bet should go to Oxfam, a charity. Oxfam received more than £100,000 from this bet.'

'This seems to be an extension of Federer's compassion. But continue with your explanation of why Federer is the GOAT. I think I agree but I'm not entirely convinced.'

'Can we not say that Federer's game is a delight to watch for all those groups of people in all the areas and not just for those slotted in the player's box?'

'No disagreement there.'

'Not only this, Federer's greatness stretches even beyond his tennis career. The sponsorship deal with a major casual wear company, closed in 2018, is valid for ten years beyond his retirement from tennis and one of the highest in terms of value. After Federer's retirement it appeared there was drop in TV viewership of the game; at that point Netflix produced a documentary series on tennis called Break Point, presumably to try to bring viewing figures back up. When Federer was playing, his game attracted more and more non-traditional spectators to watch: kids and grandmothers became glued to their TV sets. Why this new phenomenon? The reason is simple. It is the beauty of Federer's game. Beauty beyond compare.'

'Once again I can't disagree.'

I can see GP is not yet finished with this. He continues: 'Greatness needs to be viewed in another completely different dimension. This is the dimension of human energy both of a technical and non-technical kind. There is the energy of the player expended in playing and of the spectators spent in watching. Technically speaking Federer's game is particularly effortless.'

'That's another thing that distinguishes him from other, lesser players, I believe. Whereas as they often seem to be expending the maximum of energy, he seems to expend the minimum.'

'Yes: as he himself once said, one needs to be inventive. He has always observed the style, strengths and weaknesses of his opponent. He has used the wide variety of shots he is capable of. The backhand slice with its low bounce causes trouble to tall opponents. The forehand topspin passing shots down the line seems to bend in from outside, as he's able to impart both topspin and sidespin in a single effort. This special shot is magical and had many spectators gasping at the very sight. He invented a completely new tactic known as SABR—sneak attack by Roger—coming in off a short return, though without much success. It is about the process and not always the results.

'But the real beauty is in the non-technical dimension where the energy is visible at its purest. Another shot of equally magical quality he played was against Andy Roddick at Basel in 2002. He played a jumping smash shot from the back of the court in response to an overhead shot by Roddick. Andy had to literally throw his racket towards Federer in a sign of helplessness.'

'And acknowledgement of the sheer outrageousness of the shot. It was a sporting gesture.'

'Yes, and this shot against Roddick really encapsulates the essence of the beauty that is manifested in his game. Most of the time the media goes to great lengths to write about long rallies and long matches involving players who are physically strong and able to grind and belt with no inventiveness. Long rallies and long matches can produce pain in the neck to most of the watchers whereas Roger produces winners with least effort. This comes from a blend of his delicate shot making ability with the help of his mind's eye.'

'I notice we've used words like "compassion" and even "blessed". Do these belong to the world of tennis, which most people think of as a pretty physical, even brutal sport?'

'They may not be the words used by the tennis commentators and pundits. But we were trying to describe the state of mind of Federer when he played that great shot. You should know even a player like Nadal has used the word 'blessed'. Nadal has made interesting comments about Federer. Nadal has said when playing against Federer, he forgets his own play as he becomes drawn into observing Federer's game. 'Since I have memory, he is the one who has impressed me the most. The one who has entertained me the most. The one who has moved me the most…In the end tennis is about emotion.' 'Federer plays with joy, with barely constrained amazement at his own mastery. If happiness is fully expressive of your deepest talents, he is blessed indeed.' Managers need to understand this feel is natural and that is the right direction to look to in management.'

'From what I recall there are many other top tennis players apart from Nadal who felt honored to have played against Federer on the same court. I seem to remember that after losing against Federer at Wimbledon in 2019, the talented Italian player Matteo Berrettini came up to the net and said 'thanks for the tennis lesson, how much do I owe you?"

'Yes, and another thing we should mention is the famous topic of 'the decline of Roger Federer.' Pundits and others started speculating about this after Nadal defeated him in the 2008 Wimbledon final. Boris Becker announced that it was time for a changing of the guard. In 2011 Martina Navratilova said he would never regain the no.1 ranking. Federer has serenely paid little attention to all this media noise, and confounded all the prophets of doom when he came back from knee surgery in 2017 and won the Australian Open, and regained the no.1 ranking in 2018. In the last few years the media was thick with talk of the retirement of Federer from competitive tennis. But when journalists asked him about his plan for retirement, he was not annoyed. He said it is their function to ask these types of questions.'

We're sitting outside the guest quarters, at the table where we had breakfast earlier. The sun is now quite low in the sky and the birds are beginning to call to each other, as they prepare to roost. Even the colours of the shrubs and bushes look different in this light.

GP continues. 'We were talking about watching. Federer's 'feel' is also about watching. Watching is paying attention to what is at hand. For a tennis player it is watching the ball, not the target or the scoreboard. When the intensity in watching is there, everything is seen more sharply, and there seems to be more time.'

'This is connected to what I said about Federer's backhand, how he's still watching the ball, or where the ball has been, milliseconds after it has left his racket. He has so much confidence in his technique. All his attention is on 'watching the ball.' But how does this relate to management, GP?'

'Entrepreneurs get caught up in outcome rather than process. And for investors, outcome is everything. It appears Federer doesn't mind the outcome—where the ball has gone—but only the process, the doing of it. The entrepreneur needs to be aware of outcome but not caught up in it. Also, the kind of watching we are talking about with Federer cannot be outsourced. No outside agency can deliver this to you. But the key thing is keeping one's eye on the ball, which is watching. This attention or watching is moment to moment. This feel, watching the ball, cannot be taught or outsourced. Similarly core of management cannot be taught. This is one's own state of mind from moment to moment. But one can learn only by being aware.'

'But entrepreneurs can also learn from Federer about doing something for the joy, the passion of it. As he has said, he never approached tennis as a 'job'. It's a way of living. And this applies as much to the way he speaks, gives interviews, as to the way he plays.'

There is another pause. 'Perhaps', I continue, 'it's even more than a way of living, GP. It's a way of being. Of being aware. The watching or attention is to one's own mind from moment to moment. The court is the Court of Attention.'

'In case of Roger Federer this feel is palpable even to the spectators. How the division between the player and the racket, racket and the ball, ball and the court seems to dissipate. Federer seems to become the racket, the ball and the court. There is no duality. What seems to exist is only the state of watching. In the state of watching is the love of what one is doing and not getting caught up in the outcome. At the heart is timelessness and the absence of duality. For the tennis player, you and the ball are not separate. You have the court in the palm of your hand. There is no watcher and no watched but a state of pure watching.

'Watching Federer is watching beauty which is not just on the surface. There is a deeper beauty as well. There is something more important than winning, a lesson here for managers. Of course, Federer is also human. At the end of the 2009 Australian Open final, he cried. This is also relevant to managers: we are all human and flawed, even the 'greatest.'

'He can teach us also about vulnerability and humility. In one interview he said 'I always feel like my opponent has a chance. If there are days when I'm not playing well… I might lose. I know that this can happen any day.'

There are lessons there, including for sales managers.'

# 12

# Role Models

*And second-hand human beings*

---

Feeling energetic, and perhaps inspired by our reflections on Roger Federer, GP and I have started the day with an early morning game of tennis on the blue courts. It's a sunny morning, but as usual at this time of the year quite cool with a delectable freshness in the air. The birds of course have been up before us, and their morning chorus is quietening as we practise our strokes. Just once or twice I feel I've managed to channel the spirit of the great man with a passable backhand, keeping watching, trusting the process not outcome.

We have breakfast back at the guest quarters. Sitting outside, as the day begins to feel noticeably warmer, we embark on another topic. This time I kick off.

'I've noticed, GP, that entrepreneurs often cite role models—other entrepreneurs, or even figures from outside the business world, whom they greatly admire, or even idolize. And I suppose the role model most often cited is Steve Jobs. Is that a healthy thing in your view?'

GP looks thoughtful. 'To decide that we need to understand what we mean by role model. And whether looking to role models is not a sign of second-hand mind. But you're certainly right: many entrepreneurs do indeed look to role models, and especially a successful man like Steve Jobs can be at the top of the list of role models. It's a little bit like religion—some people jump in without thinking whether they can swim or not. You could take the case of Elizabeth Holmes, the founder of Theranos. She made no secret of her idolatry of Jobs: she even dressed like him, in black turtleneck tops and so on. In Silicon Valley she was known as the female version of Steve Jobs.'

'And that didn't work out particularly well. It turned out her whole enterprise—an apparently revolutionary blood-testing technology—was based on lies. I believe she's serving quite a long jail sentence for fraud. Was that inevitable? Was it clearly wrong to choose Jobs as a role model? He seems an interesting figure…'

'Ah yes, I regard Steve Jobs as one of the two most fascinating phenomena to come out of America, together with Hollywood cinema. You could say he's the most successful businessman in history, or at least in the last half-century or so.'

'But not a good role model?'

'The question is not about good or bad role model. We have to go back to the question, what is a role model? And why have a role model? For a start, we could say looking to a role model is looking to an image, not a reality. Put in another way it is like looking for inspiration. But inspiration is like a drug. The effect evaporates by next morning and you may find yourself in deep sea surrounded by whales and sharks with the distance to both shores being equal. Inspiration is a mere sensation that is transient and any edifice built on transient foundation is bound to crumble. As with Holmes copying Jobs' style of dress, as if that in itself could make her a great entrepreneur. If we are thinking about Steve Jobs, we need to think about who he really was, what made him tick, his personality, his conditioning—all those layers of mind we discussed on the road trip.'

'So who was Steve Jobs?'

'I think one has to start with the fact that he was adopted. Though he loved his adoptive parents and referred disparagingly to his birth parents as 'a sperm and egg bank', the feeling of having been abandoned never really left him. The well-researched and well-written biography titled 'Steve Jobs' by Walter Isaacson, former editor of Time magazine, seems to give a full and credible picture. So we are using that work as the basis for some of our observations about Steve Jobs. Isaacson relates that Steve Jobs' colleague Del Yocam said, 'I think his desire for complete control of whatever he makes derives directly from his personality and the fact that he was abandoned at birth.' On the other hand, Greg Calhoun, a friend of Jobs, believed that being abandoned 'made him independent. He followed the beat of a different drummer, and that came from being in a different world than he was born into.' Jobs himself had no truck with the idea that he had been traumatized by being abandoned at birth: 'Knowing I was adopted may have made me feel more independent, but I have never felt abandoned. I've always felt special. My parents made me feel special."

'And it may be, unconsciously, that this abandonment was at play when he fathered a child with Chrisann Brennan and initially failed to acknowledge it. He was repeating the trauma he himself had suffered. At that time he was the same age that his biological father was when he abandoned his mother.'

'There is a very definite distinction between responsible for and being responsible. Being responsible for implies a direction, a directed will. But the feeling of responsibility implies responsibility for everything, not in a direction, in any one particular direction. Responsible for education, responsible for politics, responsible the way I live, to be responsible for my behaviour. It's a total feeling of complete responsibility which is the ground in which action takes place.'

— *Friend on the Bench*[1]

The Bluetooth speaker on the table begins to vibrate. Panna has something to contribute. 'It is important to know the distinction between 'being responsible' and 'being responsible for'. If one is responsible per se then the second thing called 'responsible for' is naturally included. This denial of parenthood speaks of the quality of responsibility of Steve Jobs.'

'That is very true, dear Panna. But Jobs was clever as he made sure a settlement with Chrisann Brennan was signed before the IPO of Apple took place. And Jobs, by all accounts, could be cruel, sharp and tyrannical, and lacking in empathy: engaged one moment and then completely disengaged. And although in certain ways he was an exceptionally clear thinker he could also be extremely muddled. This appeared in his personal life when he seemed very unclear on the subject of relationships.'

'Say more GP.'

'For instance, Isaacson tells some fascinating stories about the writing of the biography, and why Jobs wanted it written. When Isaacson asked him this, Jobs' reply was that he wanted his kids to know him. He admitted he hadn't always been there for them. Also, when he became sick, he realized that other people would write about him and likely get the story wrong. For two years, while Isaacson was writing the book, Jobs did not question him about what was going to be included in it. He realized he might not like it but allowed Isaacson to continue with the task.'

'That does seem admirable. I gather also that he liked to pose surprise questions to managers—to catch them off guard.'

'I regard that also as a plus point, as someone caught off guard is more likely to speak the truth.'

'How about his interest in 'spirituality', his visit to India, and so on, GP? How do you evaluate that?'

'On the one hand he had a serious interest in Zen Buddhism, but it does not seem to have penetrated his psychological structure.

I am judging here by his behavior towards others which included his colleagues at work and outsiders like suppliers. He appeared to be working towards achieving his fame at any cost.

'He did realize that people in rural India rely more on their intuition rather than intellect as they do in the West. But his behaviour towards people sometimes bordered on cruelty; Jobs used to justify this by saying he needed to be honest.'

'Hmmm. I am not sure I am convinced.'

'On another topic, much of Apple's success is attributed to its development of a Graphic User interface. Crucial to this was the deal Steve Jobs made with the Xerox Corporation in Palo Alto. As Isaacson tells it, 'The Apple raid on Xerox PARC is sometimes described as one of the biggest heists in the chronicles of industry. Jobs occasionally endorsed this view, with pride. As he once said, 'Picasso had a saying—'good artists copy, great artists steal"—and we have always been shameless about stealing great ideas."

'And I seem to remember that another of Jobs's maxims was 'It's better to be a pirate than to join the navy." The Bluetooth speaker rumbles again. 'He knew the language of the Pirate's Gospel too well,' growls Panna. From what I can tell, as time went on and Apple evolved, Jobs seems to have succeeded in writing his own Gospel in the name of spirituality. God knows what is meant by spirituality here. Some of the most successful businesses seem to follow the 'Pirate's Gospel'. This whole idea of going to India, the Himalayas, Tibet for meditation and mindfulness is grossly misconstrued. There are many tech entrepreneurs who believe this is a good thing to recharge your batteries and be more successful in business. This is a tragedy of the world.'

We pause to take in what Panna has said. Then I recall something: 'Another story related by Isaacson concerns the bending of reality that happened around Jobs. When he changed the soft drinks in the refrigerator at the Apple offices to organic juices, in the early days, one employee had some t-shirts printed with the words 'Reality Distortion Field' on the front and 'It's in the juice' on the back. The phrase came from an episode of Star Trek where the aliens use willpower to bring about a new world. 'It was dangerous to get caught in Steve's distortion field,' commented another employee, "but it was what led him to actually be able to change reality."

'Whether or not Steve Jobs could change reality,' GP retorts, 'he certainly believed he was special or enlightened—one of those rare geniuses in world history like Einstein or Gandhi. Perhaps this was the positive aspect of having been abandoned and adopted. But it is not a characteristic that should be imitated, especially by people who are not special at all.'

'Perhaps Elizabeth Holmes also believed she was special,' I put in. 'Apparently she quoted Martin Luther King, "take the first step in faith".'

A burst of laughter comes from the speaker: 'The first step is the last step', booms Panna. 'It's not just about seeing the whole staircase, but about seeing inside yourself with clarity. Otherwise it could be a sudden fall and you may end up as a heap of broken bones at the foot of the staircase.'

'Or like Elizabeth Holmes serving an eleven-year jail sentence.' I ponder this for a moment. 'About being enlightened, don't I remember reading that Jobs sought enlightenment with gurus in India? Was that just part of the Zeitgeist, the kind of fad that many people were following in the 1970s?'

'Not just in the 1970s. Many entrepreneurs in the 21st century have also made the trip to India or Tibet seeking 'enlightenment', which for them meant becoming a billionaire. It was more serious than that for Steve Jobs. He went to India with a certain genuineness of intention. He took on board various aspects of 'spirituality' from gurus, especially Baba Ram Dass (born Richard Alpert). One of them related to hygiene. He became convinced that he only needed to wash once a week. The people around him found this far from enlightened or enlightening.'

'That could relate to the village godman you were talking about before, GP. Uncleanliness is next to godliness, to coin a phrase. But to cut to the chase, if you'll permit me, it sounds as if Steve Jobs was a thoroughly strange and eccentric, though also undoubtedly brilliant, man. If you don't have these qualities of Steve Jobs, forget about this role model business. You are not the same person. You are different. So don't you think just being yourself is a wise thing?'

'Yes, he was in some respects brilliant. His ideas of integrating software and hardware, and indeed the feel for the completely integrated product, were revolutionary. Bill Gates never thought the former would work but was eventually forced to admit he'd been wrong. Jobs inherited from his adoptive father the idea that the unseen parts of a product should be as beautifully designed and engineered as the visible ones.'

'The relationship between Jobs and Gates was rather interesting, was it not?'

'They were in many respects opposites. Jobs went to the very alternative Reed College in Oregon, dropped out and dropped back in. Gates went to Harvard with extremely high SAT scores, though he also dropped out—but for different reasons. Gates was a skilled computer programmer; Jobs was not. The two men, born in the same year but very different in temperament, had a stormy relationship. Issacson tells an interesting story: on one occasion, Jobs summoned Gates to Cupertino to accuse him of ripping off Apple's technology for Microsoft's Windows OS. 'I trusted you and now you're stealing from us!' shouted Jobs. Gates' reply has been quoted many times: 'Well, Steve, I think there's more than one way of looking at it. I think it's more like we both had this rich neighbor named Xerox and I broke into his house to steal the TV set and found out that you had already stolen it."

'Dr. Gonzalez. Climb to the summit and look, or do you prefer to go to bed and beg me to describe it to you? Would you be satisfied with my description? Then you have no substance, then you are a second-hand human being.'

– *Friend on the Bench*[2]

I'm lost in thought for a while. 'I suppose Gates and Jobs are two of the most admired men in America, maybe on the planet, in recent times. Yet this is not a very edifying exchange. But we were talking about role models, and, as you said near the beginning, whether following a role model isn't an indication of second-hand mind. So what is first-hand mind?'

'Here is a simple explanation of first-hand and second-hand mind. Let us say someone's thinking is based on what others are thinking and their doing on what others are doing. This person may have no understanding of the basis of what he is doing because he is simply imitating what others are doing. If, instead, he has his own understanding of the basis of what he is doing then that could be considered first-hand. It is like tasting gelato yourself and feeling the taste, as opposed to someone just describing the taste to you. Someone describes the gelato without truly tasting it: this is what a second-hand mind does. In that case it's just words.'

'And it strikes me, going back to that story about Dr Gonzalez, that it's not just a question of looking outside at the mountain top. Isn't it even more important, as we've discovered during this journey, to look inside at the same time, at the workings of one's own mind?'

GP ponders for a moment. 'Ultimately, HC, it is about understanding oneself—how one's personality is made up of a cocktail of influences, social, political, religious and so on. The influences are so various that the result is never going to be quite the same, day to day. We could also call these the layers of the mind, or the layers of conditioning.'

'The influences from our childhood may be the deepest of all, and may sometimes remain hidden. That seems to have been the case with Steve Jobs to some extent—the true effect of his having been abandoned at birth.'

'But knowing the story of Steve Jobs is only of limited value. It helps one to understand the extent and scope of human possibilities.

But unless we understand our own mind, moment by moment, we may find ourselves heading in entirely the wrong direction, like Elizabeth Holmes. It is like the blind leading the blind. So what we must do, as managers or just as human beings, is not to copy others but to understand and to watch and see ourselves as we act and react. Then maybe we will achieve a measure of clarity, which partially eluded Steve Jobs, and completely eluded Elizabeth Holmes.'

# 13

# Investors

*Illusions, damned illusions and investor's dreams*

---

It's now late morning, with the sun high in the sky and the birds quiet. 'Can you share your experience of investors, GP? I know you had some major investors from UK and US including a world's top ranking investor from US. I gather they're pretty much essential, when a business needs to expand, or get to a certain scale, but that's about all I know.'

'You're right HC in that entrepreneurs often look to investors as a panacea or solution to their problems. But they may neglect to understand the nature of investors. What are they? What are they made of? How should an entrepreneur set about choosing an investor? What are the complexities of dealing with investors? How do they exit?'

'Lots of questions there GP. And I don't have the answers to any of them.'

'Look at it this way: The nature of investors is managing other people's money. The nature of an entrepreneur is managing his enterprise. That, ideally, is a way of living in a deep sense. There is an old Roman saying, 'pecunia non olet'—money doesn't smell. So money is the same whatever its source; only the personality is different. Will the investor try to understand the personality of the entrepreneur, or just the product of the company? Do they even think that distinction is important?

'Similarly do the entrepreneurs try to understand the investors or do they ignore the personality of investors, as money has no smell? Once a US investor, whose claim to fame is a big return he earned for a petty amount invested in Google in its early days, approached us for investing. But his vision of the growth of the business in no way matched ours. So it didn't take much time to reject his offer of investment. Sometimes when investors earn huge returns, one wonders if they ever imagined making such returns. It could be like winning the jackpot. But this kind of one-trick wonder can make them go around the investment world with flying colours. An intelligent entrepreneur can see through this.'

'I can see the relationship may well be based on unstable foundations. Explain more.'

'The focus of investors is different from that of entrepreneurs. The focus of investors is on exit and outcome—the pure financial return—while the focus of entrepreneurs is on what is in their hand. They must keep their eye on the ball, not the outcome (the score). In the same way the tennis player must be aware of the score but not caught up in it.'

'So what you're saying is that the crucial part of dealing with investors is balancing the contradictory situations of how the investor is caught in the outcome whereas for the entrepreneur the work of the company is his way of living.'

'Exactly right, HC. Dealing with the complexities of business is at one level and on top of that dealing with the concerns of the investors is at another level. This is a great balancing act an entrepreneur is expected to play. If an entrepreneur does not know or is not comfortable with this balancing he and his business is sure to get into trouble. After all it is investors who are putting fuel for the journey. Without this there is no real journey. How he does all this without being caught in the outcome is the challenge. "Be aware but not be caught in it" seems to be the mantra. But having investors is imperative for any new tech company as it is they who put in fuel for the journey.

'Investors have great expectations of returns on their investment. Normally they expect to earn multiples of their investments and not a mere percentage on their investment. This is obvious as not all their investments return money; some of them may be failures. When the venture succeeds their expectations rise high.'

'Am I not right, GP, in thinking that a typical question asked by investors is 'what is the vision of the entrepreneur'?'

'You are right, HC; having a vision for the business is natural and important but it is more important not to have visionary illusions. Entrepreneurs should know that process is important and if they pay attention to this the outcome will naturally be good and not the other way around. Investors don't always know or even understand this. But there are exceptions.'

'Give me an example.'

'Take Mike Markkula, an investor in the early days of Apple, who also played a significant role in creating Apple as a company. Steve Jobs considered him as his guide to managing the business of Apple. As Walter Isaacson relates in his biography of Jobs, Jobs said "[Mike's] values were much aligned with mine". He emphasized that you should never start a company with the goal of getting rich. Your goal should be making something you believe in and making a company that will last.' But having investors like Mike Markkula is only a matter of luck and not something that can happen frequently.'

'I can imagine that.'

'There's another point we need to consider. During the last decade the valuation of companies—or the whole approach to the valuation of companies—has undergone a paradigm shift. First it was the Dotcom boom when eye balls were valued. Then came the social media companies where 'number of subscribers' came to the fore. Emphasis on future earning potential overtook every other factor. Investors and for that matter many entrepreneurs seem to have taken the Amazon growth model to follow in valuing businesses.'

'That sounds dangerous. Not every company is going to be like Amazon.'

'Indeed. This idea seems to have been stretched a bit too far. Conventionally speaking, it is earnings per share that used to be main parameter in valuing the company. Public markets used to follow the simple bench mark of size and growth of topline and profits. But in the last decade unlisted companies acquired significance as investors started valuing them based on the 'number of subscribers' and the perceived momentum of growth. So going public—making an IPO—is not so much fancied. According to one of the media: after analysts "There is something brilliant about going public after only a few years of generating any revenue at all. The sky is the limit and history is not a guide".'

'Hmmm...'

'Multiple of topline became the yardstick in some cases. There are instances like Instagram which got acquired for one billion dollars when it had no topline and was hardly one year old. One wonders what to call this model of valuation.'

'Ah, now it's coming back to me. Didn't you tell me this model is called the topless beauty?'

'We can say that the valuation game has become a puzzle. In the case of WeWork the founder Mr Neumann attempted to address that puzzle, telling Forbes in 2017: 'Our valuation and size today are much more based on our energy and spirituality than it is on a multiple of revenue."

'And as I recall 'energy and spirituality' didn't' turn out to be reliable guides. WeWork's value as company declined dramatically.'

'Yes—we will go into that shortly. The HBO comedy series Silicon Valley brilliantly captures the game of valuation in the tech world. In one of the episodes a tech company investor goes to Tibet to practice meditation with the aim of getting back to Silicon Valley recharged and achieving great success. In fact there are books in the fiction category sold in millions talking of sages living in Himalayas who can provide wisdom and energize the tech entrepreneurs to great success and wealth.'

'What do you make of all this, GP?'

'I'd say it is a tragedy if anybody in the tech world of Silicon Valley is really inspired by this and has gone to Tibet or the Himalayas with this aim in view. It is a tragedy because an authentic visit to the Himalayas or to a meet a sage would be in order to discover the depth of life and certainly not with a motive of becoming successful and making billions of dollars.

'We can say that valuation is trickier when selling a technology company because of the difficulty of capturing all the effort, ingenuity of the key managers of the company. This is a typical problem of specialists dealing in mergers and acquisitions. But let us return to WeWork, as a classic case of illusions of both investors and the entrepreneur driving the company into the dust.'

'The image comes to my mind of a road accident when two cars collide because both the drivers fail to see or notice each other. Even if one is alert it is possible to avoid the collision.'

'Or at least you can avoid being the cause of accidents in life.'

'So tell me about WeWork.'

'WeWork is a US start-up based on the idea of providing shared workspaces for technology start-ups founded by Adam Neuman.

'Conflict exists between two false entities.'

*– Friend on the Bench*[1]

Having kicked off in 2010, by January 2019, it had reached a valuation of $47 billion but from then on its value imploded, sinking to $10 billion in early 2020 (less than the $12 billion raised from investors and in loans since 2010). An effort to float the company publicly failed dismally.

'Neumann is perhaps the highest profile — or certainly, at least, the latest — case of the visionary startup CEO who gets into trouble as the company scales, goes public, or otherwise matures. According to a media publication: a leader who is glorified to the point of excess, and their startup becomes something of "a new religious movement — a cult".

'Could you say more about this 'visionary' notion, GP?'

'In one of the documents filed with SEC by WeWork, the company had stated: 'We dedicate this to the energy of we — greater than any of us, but inside each of us. We are a community company committed to maximum global impact,' it reads. 'Our mission is to elevate the world's consciousness."

'Hmm. I think we could call this an example of entrepreneurial hubris. And it was quite swiftly followed by nemesis.'

'Yes, *The New York Times* called the company's failed effort to go public and related turmoil, 'an implosion unlike any other in the history of start-ups.' And to return to our theme, WeWork was also sustained by investment provided to Neuman by SoftBank, led by Masayoshi Son. Did Son understand the nature of the company he was investing in and vice versa?'

'Probably not. They were both driving in the dark.'

'And there's one other point I haven't mentioned. I believe we need to examine the role of non-executive directors: can the director direct the course of the journey of the company? Or is he a guinea pig? Is he offering a change of agenda or change of snack menu served during the meeting? The presence of directors on the board of public companies seems to be to provide credibility, not anything deeper.'

'I suppose a director can—sometimes at least—prevent a fraud or scam if he or she is alert.'

'Yes. But there are many cases of dumb directors who ended up as mere spectators and unable to prevent fraud. Sometimes investors seem to behave like fortune hunters or racing punters. We have mentioned the early investor in Google who made a fortune and was hailed as a genius but was more like someone who won the jackpot in the lottery, or backed a winning horse at long odds. Other investors can get the horse racing analogy wrong in another way: Ross Perot who invested in Apple had a meeting with Steve Jobs and declared that he was in. 'I pick the jockeys, and the jockeys pick the horses and ride them,' he told Jobs. 'You guys are the ones I'm betting on.' But it is not jockeys who win races. Horses win races. And finally we should always remember that exiting is one of the key preoccupations of investors. But sometimes, for some investors, exiting can be from one prison to another.'

# 14

# Employees

## *Building blocks and shifting sands*

---

In the couple of days we have left at the School in the Valley, GP and I establish a new routine. After my early morning birdwatching, followed by breakfast at our guest quarters, GP and I sit down to discuss a new theme. At some point we break for coffee darshan; we join teachers and pupils for lunch, and in the late afternoon there's a chance for tennis.

'I notice, GP, that we haven't yet discussed something rather fundamental—the question of employees. Obviously the entrepreneur can't do it entirely alone. He or she needs help—but my sense is that employees can be as much a hindrance as a help.'

'Yes, you're right HC. Here I'd like to take us back to the village. Parents often want their offspring—and their prospective sons- and daughters-in-law—to have what are sometimes called "dream jobs".'

'What does that mean?'

'Well, you know, working for a company with a famous name. That is the route to success and happiness, it is often thought.

The father-in-law wants the prospective son-in-law to be carrying the visiting card of a big-name company.'

'But the reality turns out to be somewhat different.'

'Yes. The reality is that your job is defined by the relatively small number of people you actually interact with. That doesn't really change no matter the size of the company.'

'I understand that dream jobs may be something of an illusion. But how about 'dream employees'? Does the same apply to them?'

'Sometimes, quite often in fact, employees are selected on the basis of their qualifications. They may tick all the boxes in that respect—degree from top university, MBA etc. But that does not guarantee they will make a good employee.'

'Yes, I have firsthand experience of that. Someone I know took on a partner to help run his small business—a person who could not have been better qualified on paper. But in practice he proved to be unable to fulfil the basic requirements of the job, answering customers' correspondence and queries and so on. It nearly broke this person's spirit. So how does the entrepreneur avoid these pitfalls?'

'Once again, HC, we return to the state of mind. The entrepreneur or manager must be realistic about the motivations and incentives of his or her employees. A tech company or start-up needs dedicated and committed employees, but the CEO or entrepreneur needs to be aware that employees like any other human beings are equally interested in their self-growth in terms of salary, higher positions and so on. To believe all employees are equally committed and dedicated is, shall we say, idealistic.'

'Or hopelessly naïve.'

'Yes. I would say a CEO or entrepreneur should count themselves lucky if they have three to five colleagues at the top layer of management who can relate to their state of mind. Even if the CEO has one manager who can relate to the company like him, that is the equivalent of doubling the capacity and bandwidth at the top. If the CEO has three to five key colleagues who have a similar relationship with the venture, they can form the foundation of the company. There may be others in the rest of the company, but it is up to the key managers to spot them and nurture them for the long term. Otherwise, no one should be surprised that most employees always look for greener pastures and keep switching their jobs. The key challenge of building a sustainable company for the long term is the balance between the employees who form the major building blocks and others who are essentially jumping jacks.'

'You're saying that these employees become indispensable. But I guess there's a risk in that. What happens if they leave all the same? And won't they take all the company secrets with them?'

'You're absolutely right there HC. There's no doubt that key employees become intellectual property risks.'

## Limitations of HR function

'As we're talking about employees, it strikes me, GP, that every company of any size has a whole department devoted to their welfare—the HR department.'

'Ah yes, the famous Human Resources. HR has its function, but it's a very limited and technical function. The role of HR lies in maintaining the technical aspects of employment such as records of appointment, salary records, leave records etc.'

'Some managers expect too much from HR—is that what you're saying?'

'Yes. Think about it this way. The core function of management is managing the employees and this is performed by the immediate line manager. This cannot be outsourced. As we've discussed, this is not a technical task. HR can be a barrier in this process.'

'Explain.'

'Who is the person who observes the whole conduct of the team member in the office—the way he or she responds to the daily routine and to crisis situations? Is it the manager or the head of HR?'

'Well of course it's the manager. And as we've discussed—and as we learned right at the beginning—this is more a matter of feel, like the feel Panna had for his animals, than of technical knowledge. So I can imagine the technical knowledge of the head of HR might be hindrance not a help.'

'Precisely.'

## Recruitment and biodata managers

There's a pause.

'I believe there's more to be said on the subject of recruitment. The weapon of choice used by the prospective employee is their biodata, or what used to be called curriculum vitae.'

'And you're going to tell me that not everything on the CV should be taken at face value. Indeed, I recall certain English Conservative politicians who turned out to have invented large parts of their CVs.'

'One thing is outright invention. That shouldn't be too difficult to spot. But another is what you might call 'resumé padding'.'

'Inflated claims? Meaningless verbiage?'

'That and worse.'

'And what is the solution?'

'Direct questioning at interview which cuts to the chase can be very helpful. Sometimes even the use of 'curveball' questions as raised by Steve Jobs, who asked one candidate whether he was a virgin. Of course asking this kind of question verges on the eccentric and we are not recommending this. And in this area we can draw attention to the birth of new businesses like CV Validation services.'

'One thing is recruiting. But presumably employees have to be appraised on a regular basis, GP. Annual reviews and so on…

'Oh yes, there are many stories about that. The fear and trembling.'

'It sounds as if you have another approach.'

'Indeed. Instead of the pain of yearly appraisals, which create nervousness for no reason, in my company we have always believed in frank appraisal as and when it happens. That has many advantages. There is no unnecessary time lag for a start. If there's a problem, why put off the solution for a year? That makes no sense, either for the employee or the company.'

## Delegation and trust

'As a complete novice in this area, GP, it strikes me that surely for a manager one of the most important and difficult issues can be delegation. I've known very capable people who seemed entirely incapable of delegation.'

'Of course, HC, there are no end of formulaic books, gallup studies and similar things, dedicated to the subject of delegation.'

'Eight steps to effective delegation, that kind of thing?'.

'Yes, but they never ask what is at the core of delegation.'

'I suppose trust has a lot to do with it. You can only delegate effectively if you can trust the person you are delegating the work to.'

'Exactly. And what is trust? A state of mind. If we look at delegation more carefully we can say it consists of the handing over of functional work with requisite authority to the right person. But it absolutely does not consist of abdication of responsibility. Responsibility cannot be delegated. However the sense of responsibility is not the personal preserve of the manager only—the person who delegates. It is also desirable that the delegate is a man or woman of responsibility.'

'How can you choose or have a sense of who is the right person?'

'One thing we can be sure of is that if the action of delegation is more laborious than the work itself then it is a case of total failure.'

'And that quite often happens, I believe. Managers end up doing the work twice, because they can't trust the other person to do it properly.

'The second most important thing is the addition of value by the colleague, let us call him an assistant for the moment, in the discharge of the delegated function. Is the assistant adding to the load of the already congested mind of the manager or reducing the load? These two factors become acid tests.'

'That seems clear. But I'm not sure we've got to the core of it, which in this case is the nature of trust. We can agree that delegation is one of the key functions of management, and delegation requires trust. But does the manager understand what trust is?'

'You've put your finger on it, HC. To trust someone else, how is it possible unless the manager himself or herself understands what trust is? Before putting that question if he or she understands what trust is, the manager needs to ask himself or herself if he or she is trustworthy or untrustworthy. Not trust for any specific purpose. But trust per se. If this is all too much to understand he or she can ask himself or herself a simple question: is he or she trustworthy in his or her most intimate relationship. Only when he or she understands how untrustworthy he or she is then it may be possible to trust someone else. Out of this understanding of untrustworthiness emerges trust. That understanding can help one to act and delegate rightly. If you think you have a bit of untrustworthiness be prepared to think that your ability to understand the other employee in terms of delegation could also be defective to that extent.'

# 15

# Sales Management

## *Sense of wonderment*

---

GP has a few more areas of management he wants to discuss with me, I gather. When he lists them as sales management, finance management and productivity, I feel somewhat daunted. We are sitting, for a change, under the big banyan tree.

'These sound like technical areas, GP. I'm not sure what I can contribute here.'

'They sound technical, HC, I agree. But I suspect they will turn out to have more than a little to do with what we have been discussing up to now.'

'Say more.'

'In business there is a truth of the matter or core of selling if one can call it that: the customer is always right. if you think the customer is wrong then you are in the wrong business, or at least with a wrong customer. If most of the customers are wrong, then surely you are in the wrong business. The salesman should be aware of the state of mind of a customer; one customer represents most of the customers. That is why so much value is attributed to a reference sale and the valuation of the company significantly changes.

'A large part of the problem may be an overtechnical approach. So many salespeople approach their work as if it were a technical challenge.'

'I'm sure many books have been written on sales technique. But if it's not a technical challenge, what is it?'

'Here we need to understand the operations of the mind in the moment. This becomes the key challenge to both the CEO and to the salesman. Generally sales is not an easy function, especially when you have strong competition. So the skill of the salesperson is to channel his or her energies intelligently to pursue a pipeline of hopeful opportunities. During a review meeting when confronted with questions by the CEO, the salesperson normally resorts to explanations of the delay in his or her efforts to achieve a sales target. In the process he or she may not be aware the operations of his or her own mind which most of the times tries to suppress or escape. Similarly this also poses a challenge to the CEO to see through the explanations and get to the fact of the matter.'

'Which might not be easy at all.'

'Setting a marketing budget is a typical annual exercise. Unfortunately this is taken for granted by many sales and marketing people. A CEO needed to educate his or her marketing manager that the word 'Budget' typically applies to a government function whose main function is to collect revenues and spend the money for public purposes. So resources are allocated against various public projects such as new initiatives in health, education, irrigation, some public welfare schemes etc. A CEO typically questions the marketing manager on the need for allocating resources for the budget. The marketing manager must then explain every item of expenditure, the need for it, implications and the significance of each item.'

'Why do you think this CEO has to go through this routine matter with so much rigor, GP?'

'I think that is the right thing to do, in other words to let the marketing manager pay attention to everything he or she is speaking about, not skim over it without paying attention. It is all about the state of mind. The CEO does not want the Marketing Manager to take things for granted. You could compare it to shaving which becomes a habit for most males to go through every morning. If instead of making it a habit, you start paying attention to what you are doing, then there is depth to the process: you focus on what you are doing and the right way to do it. Otherwise the result can be a sloppy mind.'

'Yes, and that can surely apply to other areas of life.'

## Sense of wonderment

'Now I'd like to go somewhere quite different. When I was a child, growing up in the village, like all children I suppose, I had a great sense of curiosity, especially about any people from outside who came to visit. We would wait around by the bus-stop, in the centre of the village, to see who would get off. It was more than curiosity, actually; I'd call it wonderment.'

'I remember feeling that too. I'm afraid in my case it was more birds and insects than humans that I was curious about. But I always think of that line spoken by Miranda in Shakespeare's Tempest, when she sees the shipwrecked arrivals on her father Prospero's island: "Oh brave new world, that has such people in it!" She has seen so few people that she thinks they are all wonderful. She really means it.'

'And it's so important for the salesperson to keep that sense of wonderment—to have an open, fresh and quiet mind. Quiet mind above all, so there is space.'

'I suppose having too much technique or theory can get in the way. Then your mind is full of technique and theory, and you do not see what is in front of you.'

'There are gurus and masters who think they can teach a technique or two and make some good money in the process, for successful selling. But much of it is common sense if one approaches it from the angle of the state of mind of the salesperson. Let us see how the state of mind works while fixing the marketing budget, or in the preparation of a salesperson before approaching a customer.'

'Even before—coming from what we said about suitability to the job—one could ask if this person has a flair for selling things or not.'

'Exactly, HC. You have hit the nail on the head. If you take the example of a software programmer, they are more comfortable with their technical job of software programming. They are not the type of person who enjoys travelling to meet customers. There's a story of a CEO of a company that had developed best-in-class products going to many countries in Europe to sell his product. Since this was a very technical product, he had to take his technology chief to make presentations to customers. At the end of their trip the CEO thought that the tech chief must be very happy that he'd had a chance to see the world. But to his surprise the tech chief remarked that he hadn't learned anything new at the end of the world trip, as he could not add anything to his knowledge of his programming languages.'

'I've come across people like that. They think differently from us—those of us who love travelling and seeing the world.'

'So once again, HC, what seems of paramount importance is the state of mind of the salesperson and that of the customer he or she is meeting. Normally, a salesperson prepares as thoroughly as he or she can before meeting the customer. It is much like a student preparing for his year-end exam. He or she does his best to imagine all the possible questions that they may have to face in the exam hall and still they may end up facing most unexpected questions.'

'I've been there myself.'

'Once my friend was accompanied by a senior manager to a customer visit. It was an important meeting as it was potentially the first sale of their new product, and the customer had a high reference value for subsequent sales. The senior manager was overly concerned and was rather tense about what kind of questions the customer would pose. He was very much like the kind of college student who is mugging and cannot stop reading and rereading the book until he or she enters the exam hall. My friend suggested to him it would be better to stop preparing and keep his mind empty before entering the meeting with the customer, watch the anxiety in his own mind and also observe the state of the mind of the customer. Because you never know if that day the customer has had a painful encounter with his wife or children at home or a humiliating meeting with his boss in the office. Or if he has already made up his mind in favour of the competitor.'

'So what you're saying, GP, is that it's essential for the salesperson to pause before entering the meeting, to feel the atmosphere in the meeting room of the customer. And to gauge the state of his or her own mind.'

'Exactly, HC. Is his mind filled with the techniques of selling or is he also looking at the customer—how the customer is looking at him, if he is offering a cup of coffee or tea, is he able to savour the coffee, how the customer is keeping his desk, how he is behaving towards his colleagues and subordinates? Good luck to the salesperson if the customer does not seem to have their life in order and still buys the product.

'There are instances when the salesperson needs to be very frank and honest especially when facing the meaningless approaches of some customers. There are customers who derive great pleasure in showing off their knowledge and one-upmanship. There are also accumulators of knowledge who have no intention of buying the product. If the customer happens to be the CTO or any of his team members, you may also see a tendency for them to enrich their CV by buying well established brands. Adding this work experience to their CV can help them when they look for a job change. There are also customers who think very highly of your competitors' products for superficial reasons and bargain you down. I can tell a story about one Mr. Gats Pump, a tall and impactful talker, marketing a me-too product. He was known in the industry as he happened to be a regular speaker in many international conferences. He also was grooming Mr. New Pump, his son, to succeed him in his business. One of the customers seems to have been very enamoured with this tall and talkative gentleman and kept quoting him in the conversation. He went so far as to tell us that Mr. Gats Pump was the father of tower engineering. Then the salesperson realized that the chances of a successful sale here were not high, and allowed himself a spontaneous response. He suggested to the customer that he might be overstating the value of Mr. Gats Pump by elevating him to the level of a figure such as Galileo, often called the father of observational astronomy and one of the founders of modern science. The salesperson was fairly sure that Gats Pump had done no such pathbreaking work: he had merely developed a mediocre product with the help of some college students free of cost. The salesperson ended up informing the customer that as far as he knew Gats Pump was the father of his son New Pump. That and no more.'

'That reminds me of some words of the Friend on the Bench: "Is technique driving the sales process or is moment of life driving the process in its own lively style?"'

That seems the moment for a pause, and to tune in again with where we are, our own moment of life.

Then GP resumes. 'You can also sum it up more simply still: the logic of sales is the logic of business.'

'What do you mean by that?'

'Well, first of all, the salesperson must believe in the product. If he or she does not believe in the product, how can they sell it with any conviction?'

'I have heard an American tennis player say 'fake it till you make it', but that approach does not make sense to me. It sounds too effortful.'

'Indeed.'

I try to sum up. 'So our conclusion is that it all comes down, again, to attention to the state of mind. For the salesperson to be aware of his or her own state of mind, and also, as far as possible, that of the customer. If the salesperson is too preoccupied with sales techniques, or is over-prepared, they will not be aware of the customer's state of mind, of what is happening in that moment. The salesperson needs to recapture that sense of wonderment we all had as children, when we were so curious about each new person we came across.'

## Salesperson's equilibrium

'Rather than frantically mugging up like a nervous student, the salesperson can take a nap in the reception area where she could be kept waiting for the customer to call her in. A salesperson is normally nervous before she gauges the intention of the customer. Until then the waiting time she spends in the reception area of the customer is generally filled with tension. But the tension evaporates when she understands for sure the customer is buying her product. This is the moment she can wait in the reception area of the customer in a relaxed state, and can even afford to take a nap in the sofa of the reception while waiting to be called in. This is the moment of Salesperson equilibrium. If a customer is openly critical of your product, take that as a benefit. Then there is no more illusion of a sale and energies of a salesperson are not wasted any more. She could pursue some other sales opportunity.'

After a pause I have another thought. 'One thing that's always intrigued me about salesmanship is those enormous 'coffee table' sales brochures you sometimes see, say in a company waiting room. What are they good for?'

GP chuckles. 'Some of them are big enough to occupy the entire width and length of the table. And don't try to pick them up—they might give you tennis elbow. I have a story to tell involving a very large-sized brochure. An MRI scanner is a big ticket item, as the cost of each scanner could be in the range of half a million to one million dollars. Once a salesman was carrying a very big size brochure for an MRI scanner. This salesman had a great sense of humour. When asked why such a big size brochure his response was that no trash bin in the world could accommodate the brochure.

'These brochures are full of product information and other research and specifications. Who reads all this? Probably mostly competitors, who gain valuable information about the company's products and references.'

## WWW—Right time to exit?

GP is looking rather mischievous. 'Do you know about WWW, or the three w's, HC?'

'I assume you're not referring to the worldwide web, GP?'

'No, this is my own little acronym. W is for work. Whatever kind of business we're in, whether it's tech or something else, we must make the product work. That will help with selling it.'

'That seems uncontroversial.'

'But the product will not sell on its own. So we come to the second w, which is word. We need marketing experts, wordsmiths—like you HC—to communicate the story of the product.'

'So far so good. I sense a sting in the tail.'

'It is coming. So the third w is wine, women and song. These are various stages of the evolution of business. It means as the business keeps growing in size, ultimately you face a moment of reckoning. The final W stands for companies who are pitching to gain billion dollar businesses from customers. It implies you need to compete with big multinational giants.'

'Where do they come into it?'

'It is rumoured that some big companies provide blacked-out stretch limos, with suitable entertainment, for favoured customers. At this point it is time for an entrepreneur, any sensitive human being, to exit the business.'

'In other words, sometimes you may be up against competition that is simply out of your league. I read the other day that an aviation company made an out-of-court settlement for bribery offences of 3.6 billion euros in penalties to anti-corruption agencies in France, the UK and the US. 3.6 billion euros! That would buy a fair number of stretch limos.'

'You remember Mark Knopfler's song about the McDonalds CEO Ray Kroc, 'Boom Like That'? Let's play it now on the speaker.' GP takes out his mobile phone and taps in the song. 'My name is not Krock, that is Kroc with a K, like Crocodile but not spelled that way, it is dog eat dog, rat eat rat…'

'We must never forget, HC, that competition, by fair means or foul, is the name of the game. The background to that song is spelled out in the film 'The Founder' which depicts the story of the McDonald brothers whose business gets taken over by Ray Kroc. During the final negotiations Ray Kroc used these words 'in business, dog eat dog, rat eat rat'.'

# 16

# Finance Management

## *Finger on the pulse*

---

It's time to break for lunch. Students and teachers are coming out of class, heading for the big dining hall which serves good healthy south Indian vegetarian food—dal, rice, peas, tomatoes and so on. Some are still carrying on conversations which began in the classroom, continuing to discuss books, ideas. It's a lovely, lively scene. GP and I sit at a table with some old friends of his, including a senior administrator who completed a Doctorate in Physics and dedicated his life to the work of that School in the Valley.

After lunch we head back to the guest quarters. We're going to discuss one more topic before our late afternoon tennis.

'Now finance management—our next topic—sounds rather a technical subject to me, GP. Here you will have to enlighten me.'

'You're right, HC, in that accounting, unlike marketing, is a technical subject. That is to say, a subject that deals with numbers and not with human beings directly.'

The Bluetooth speaker has been placed on the table and it begins to vibrate. The voice of Panna speaks: 'Finance is the lifeblood of commerce. Without finance there is no business.'

'I get that, Panna.'

GP continues. 'So if finance is the lifeblood of commerce, then the Finance Manager and for that matter the CEO should be like a doctor who has his finger on the pulse. It is the touch of the pulse that can tell the doctor about one of the basic parameters of the patient's health condition. Here of course we are talking about having all the statements of numbers, as they call them in the world of investors and financial consulting.'

'So you could call it a diagnostic tool.'

'Yes, a finance manager or a CEO with good understanding of finances can feel the health of the organization by a look at these numbers, much as a doctor can feel the basic health condition of the patient by keeping his finger on his pulse. When it comes to symptoms there is a tendency wrongly to attribute everything to finance problems, just as some lay persons think their health problem is blood-related, just because blood tests are the measure of health. Accounting, as we've said, is a technical subject unlike marketing. For a business school to include Finance Management as a subject to teach is much like a business school professing to teach medicine.'

'How about Chartered Accountancy? That was your training, wasn't it GP?'

'Yes and in my view this is by far the best course to help a Finance Manager develop the feel of the numbers that make up a financial statement. This is because he starts his understanding of the subject of accounting from the very basic level of writing vouchers, cash book, ledger, drawing a trial balance, then leading up to profit and loss account, balance sheet and finally cash flow statement. He is well aware of the disorder book keeping can create. Hence his understanding of order in accounting is born out of the mess the accounting is capable of. In that sense he has the feel of the finance more directly.'

'It sounds as if for a CEO or any Senior Manager to understand financial statements is a pretty important skill.'

'Yes, but for, say, an engineer turned CEO sometimes it could be tricky to read and understand a financial statement. If you take the P&L statement which shows the revenues, expenses, profit or loss, also known as bottom line in the operations, you will have to go through many lines of data. Here the trap is one can get lost in the details easily, thus the discussion can tend to ignore the bigger picture. The cardinal principle is to see the whole first and then the details. To make matters simple you can simply divide everything into three lines—top line (all revenues), middle line (all expenses consolidated to start with) and bottom line (profit or loss). Unless the middle line total is less than the top line there is no positive bottom line. A company with a bigger (wider) middle line is like a person with a wide waist and one can imagine the shape of the body.'

'That certainly makes it easier to understand!'

## Debt collection and cash management

'With all this said, not many CEOs of tech companies truly understand the difference between profit and cash. Loss in the operations is not always a worrying thing: so also shortfall in the cash balance which sometimes has to do with collection of receivables. Nor is having too much cash balance always a good thing.'

## GIPEX models

Panna has another contribution. 'How about having a GIPEX model instead of an ageing statement? This direct language of GIPEX cannot be misunderstood by the sales guys. This terminology can serve as a tool of effective communication also'

'Explain.'

'Ageing statement of debtors is a commonplace expression in finance management. You prepare a statement showing all the money owed to your company by your customers. It is not uncommon that all customers are not prompt in paying the dues in time. So you categorize the total debts owed to your company age-wise. Depending on the terms of sale debts unpaid within, let us say 60 days in one column, 60-120 days in another column, beyond 120 days in another column. The salesperson needs to collect the old debts also that are long outstanding. This is what a good finance manager wants. But the understanding of a salesman seems to be at odds with this objective. It is obvious a Finance Manager gets annoyed when the sales manager takes pride in the collection of recent debts and neglects the oldest ones outstanding from a customer. One does not know if a salesperson is deliberately pretending not to understand the statement and the underlying intentions properly. Hence the creation of GIPEX models. As per the GIPEX model, debts paid, for instance, within 60 days go under the heading 'good', or G. 60 days to 120 day is categorized as 'infected' or I. Unpaid after 120 days is 'poisonous', P. Then you derive an Index based on the level of debts under the three categories as at the start of the year. A CEO may fix a target for collections during the year so as to maintain a balance of zero under P and say 0.5 or whatever for the category of I in comparison to the levels at the start of the year. During the year while reviewing, to get a quick grasp of the status, CEO needs to view only the total of the I and P from the perspective of the target of zero and 0.5. Of course he needs to factor in the sales level of the current year while reviewing. This model is what we have called as GIPEX model and makes things unmistakably clear to everyone involved.'

'Again, even an ignoramus like me can understand that.'

'Yes. This leaves little room for misunderstanding and escaping from the responsibility. Mind you, GIPEX is the terminology used in internal communications without sounding poisonous and not to cause bad feelings among sales and finance people.'

'That also sounds sensible, dear Panna.'

## Bean counters and petty minds

'Here's another issue that crops up, HC,' continues GP. Some CEOs can be obsessed with knowing the numbers to the last digit. This is the mindset of an accountant whose job is to tally the trial balance to the last cent. He or she knows any difference that could come up in the trial balance could be due to a major error in the accounting. So it is his or her job to do a thorough job in ensuring that all tasks involved in making the financial statements are carried out meticulously and precisely. He or she also knows that the job he or she does should stand due diligence by any reputed firm of accountants. While an accountant cannot sleep if the trial balance does not tally with a minor discrepancy of one dollar, a CEO needs to have more the feel of the business than the mindset of an accountant. As John Maynard Keyes put it, *'It is better to be roughly right than precisely wrong.'* This seems very relevant in this context.

'When it comes to accounting of expenses, this is very much governed by accounting standards as set out by accounting standards bodies internationally. Accounting of goodwill, accrued income, stock valuations fall into a grey area and arguments can be made on either side. But sometimes these practices can border on criminality. That is where the Finance Manager's ability and for that matter the ability of the CEO to have the feel of the numbers is crucial.'

Panna once again intervenes: 'Profit is a matter of policy. Cost is a matter of fact.'

GP is quiet for a moment. Then he comments, 'This statement of Panna is quite profound. Only an accountant who has the feel of the whole accounting exercise can make sense of that. It is amazing how sometimes even big professional firms miss this vital piece of understanding during the process of due diligence in Mergers and Acquisitions. For example, Hewlett Packard acquired Autonomy, a UK tech company, in 2011 for $11 bn. Subsequently Hewlett-Packard revealed that it took an $8.8bn (£5.5bn) write down after 'serious accounting improprieties' were discovered at Autonomy. This led to high-profile litigation. In September 2020, Deloitte, who audited Autonomy between 2009 and 2011, were fined £15m for audits that contained 'serious and serial failures'.'

'So you're saying it's not just the numbers but the feel of the numbers.'

'Yes.'

Panna has one final comment: 'Be aware that finance management is about the book of numbers and understanding the state of mind is about reading the book of life.'

'Indeed.'

# 17

# Productivity

*Three immutable laws*

---

There's another pause. The sun is beginning to sink towards the west now and the trees bordering the guest quarters' garden provide welcome shade. We get up and stretch our legs for a moment.

'Have I ever spoken to you, HC, about the three immutable laws?'

'Hmmm, maybe you have. Remind me.'

'They are quick action, facts and clarity. The first is quick action.'

'Ah. Perhaps not my strong point. Couldn't that be overhasty?'

'Yes, but I am not speaking about haste. Instead of in haste we should do any job in the right time. First of all we have to make some distinctions. Activity is not action.'

'Explain the difference.'

'You visit an office, and you may see people engaged in activity—apparently busy. They are probably writing internal emails; who knows, they may even be spending time on private social media. But writing internal emails is not action. It is mere activity. It may

'One can talk endlessly, describing, piling words upon words, coming to various forms of conclusions, but out of all this verbal confusion if there is one clear action that action is worth ten thousand words.'

– *Friend on the Bench*[1]

be appropriate for a customer support agent to reply to customer complaints promptly. But it could be a great fallacy for a manager to derive satisfaction at the end of the day from the fact that one has answered all the mails—even though one should always respond in time. That manager is completely unaware that he is a mere Inbox Manager.'

'Yes, there was the case of the minister in the House of Commons in London who turned out to be watching… well we won't go into that. But tell me, how do you define action?'

'Action is action in time. Time is always now. What we do today is part of what we achieve for the year. Today contains the whole of the year. So Quick Action is when we are businesslike, not ritual-like. Some people cannot distinguish between the two. So the quick action we are talking of is in the psychological domain.'

'Sometimes presumably we need time to think.'

'Indeed. A strategic matter requires time to understand, debate and brainstorm. But not matters of business as usual.'

## Facts are as they are

'You must have some basis for your quick action, I suppose, GP.'

'Of course. Actions and decisions are based on facts and not opinions.'

'So how do you define facts.'

'If we start by using the tool of negation, hearsay is not a fact. Facts are as they are. People talk about 'unpleasant facts'.'

The Bluetooth speaker vibrates. Panna has something to say: 'A fact is neither pleasant nor unpleasant. It is so. One neither accepts nor rejects a fact. One has to live with the fact.'

'Easier said than done! Some people go through their whole lives not being able to face facts. But then also facts may be not so easy to uncover. What is really going on in a business, for instance. One

'A fact can never be denied. Opinion about fact can be denied.'

– *Friend on the Bench*[2]

'A mind that gives an opinion about a fact is a narrow, limited, destructive mind ... You can translate the fact in one way, and I can translate it in another way. The translation of the fact is a curse which prevents us from seeing the actual fact and doing something about the fact. If you and I could see the fact without offering an opinion, interpreting, giving a significance, then the fact becomes much more alive—not more alive—the fact is there alone, nothing else matters; then the fact has its own energy which drives you in the right direction.'

– *Friend on the Bench*[3]

thinks of all those employees of Bernie Madoff or Elizabeth Holmes, or Sam Bankman-Fried, the well-known fraudsters. Someone must have known what was going on. But the vast majority either didn't know or didn't want to know.'

'You're quite right, HC. When I've wanted to ascertain facts, I've insisted on first-hand understanding. Go directly to the source. Nothing else substitutes for that—though it's not always possible. It is not you who makes the decision but facts that make a decision. The challenge is to let the facts emerge onto the table.'

## Clarity

There is a pause.

'And I suppose this is where clarity comes in.'

'Yes. We could say, adapting St Paul, that clarity is the greatest of these three laws. Without clarity nothing we do can hit its mark.'

'So what is clarity? How often do we achieve it?'

Panna intervenes from the speaker. 'Clarity is not confusion. Nor is it the opposite of confusion. The realization that one is confused is the beginning of clarity.'

'I like that, Panna. There's something everyone could relate to.'

'Though it takes a certain humility', adds GP. 'Think how many go on from confusion to confusion, ever deepening the confusion. As you mentioned, Bernie Madoff, Elizabeth Holmes.'

'The further we go into it, the more difficult it is to get out. As Macbeth said after the murder of Duncan, 'I am in blood/ Stepp'd in so far that should I wade no more,/ Returning were as tedious as go o'er."

'But Macbeth was wrong in thinking it was possible to 'go o'er'. If you stay in confusion you never escape from it. Clarity is the real ground upon which everything else of an orderly life is built. Clarity is action. Quick action is possible only when there is clarity. Clarity is the ground of productivity. In fact clarity is an important part of wisdom. A confused mind can be working very hard, but it does not know where it is heading and so can get caught in mere activities instead of action. A confused mind may not be aware that instead of getting to the top of the mountain it could be climbing down the hill and still may have the illusion that it is getting to the top. Or an experienced driver who does not know the route will end up driving round in circles. Similarly if you have ever observed a skilled barber who has clarity about what he is doing, he will finish the job quickly and efficiently. This is because he is clear about what he is supposed to do. On the contrary, a barber who lacks clarity in his function may take more time and also may end up messing up the job.'

Panna has one more contribution. 'Software development is a great example of action and extensions. You may be aware of some commonplace applications like Word, Excel. If you have ever worked on a word document and stored it in your computer it will have .doc as its extension.'

'Or .docx in the latest version, Panna.'

'This naming of extension is very important for accessing the file later on. Having an extension for any output of any software application is an integral part of how a software application is developed. It is the job of the management of the company to find a suitable name of the extension. So on this basis you can name the action that results out of confusion as .confusion. For instance you start a venture out of inspiration or a boy gets into a relation with a girl out of sheer sensation and without clarity; then the resulting action can be filed as .confusion (dot confusion) in one's mind.'

'What are you saying, Panna? If I take the instance of a friend of mine, the whole set of actions in his whole life can be filed as .confusion. There can be so many files.'

'In that case he can create a Zip file.'

# 18

# Beyond Business Schools

## *Nurturing the second horse*

---

It is a beautiful sunny morning at the School in the Valley. After breakfast, still sitting at the table where GP has also placed the Bluetooth speaker, we decide to return to a theme we have touched on earlier. GP starts.

'We need to check back in to the subject of business schools and the kind of education they are or are not offering.'

'That seems sensible. You had misgivings when we visited the business school in your home town a few days ago.'

'Yes, I did. I think if the current education that is offered in business schools is only about the academic side of education, the consequences are obvious. It appears that the other side of education—that is education about life itself—is completely absent in most of the educational institutions.'

'So it appears. What in fact do the business schools offer?'

'We can take as another reference an article, entitled 'How Business Schools Lost their Way', which was published in Harvard Business Review in May 2005. The co-authors were Warren Bennis, a Distinguished Professor of Management at the University of Southern California, and James O'Toole, a Professor of Business Ethics at the University of Denver's Daniels College of Business.'

'These chaps were big cheeses in their field, I gather.'

'Indeed. Bennis, who died in 2014, was an organizational consultant and author, widely regarded as a pioneer of the contemporary field of Leadership Studies. For example The Financial Times referred to him in 2000 as 'the professor who established leadership as a respectable academic field".'

'And it sounds as if the article is quite critical of Business Schools.'

'Yes. You could say his article is a credit to the editorial minds of HBR: hats off to them for publishing such a critical piece about business schools when their own affiliate Harvard Business School is a top-ranking name in business education worldwide.'

'So what did Bennis and O'Toole have to say for themselves?'

'The article, as mentioned, was titled "How Business Schools Lost Their Way".' It started off saying that 'Business Schools are on the wrong track'.

'I think we can agree on that.'

'Some of the points are certainly valid, though the article loses track of the reality of the business world as it goes along. It says that business is not run on scientific models.'

Here the Bluetooth speaker begins to vibrate. 'I agree,' interposes Panna. 'Business cannot be run on scientific models. Business is not mathematics. It is not linear. It is non-linear and dynamic.'

'Indeed, Panna,' agrees GP. 'And the article argued the importance of facts and integration. Employers of these MBAs became aware of the shortcomings of the courses in Business Schools, related to the fact that the professors who teach the students have no practical experience. The article had an excellent analogy: 'we cannot imagine a professor of surgery who has never seen a patient, or a piano teacher who doesn't play the instrument, and yet today's business schools are packed with intellectual faculty with little or no managerial experience.' The article reserves its most stinging comment for the conclusion where it says, "By allowing the scientific research model to drive out all others, business schools are institutionalizing their own irrelevance."

'But the writers of this article don't seem to be aware of the ground realities of the business world. That much is obvious if you look at the kinds of solution they prescribe to the maladies of business education. 'Make the world a better place' is the motto of many so-called leading business schools in the world. A commitment to public good is no doubt a good thing to have, but it must be grounded in business reality.'

'So many of those slogans are just empty guff, I fear.'

'Yes, and the article concludes with suggestions under the title 'Looking ahead' stressing the value of cognitive science and neuroscience for business education. So while saying the business schools should not ignore the value of studies in humanities, the article replaces one technique-based approach with another technique-based approach, as it advocates usage of magnetic resonance imaging technology to study how the brain behaves while making economic decisions.'

'Would that be helpful in the moment of making a decision, I wonder?'

'The role of trust was also mentioned but it was only a passing comment and the article does not explore it in depth. All of this appears to be completely out of tune with the way to understand the workings of the mind, as we have discussed it, does it not HC?'

Once again the Bluetooth speaker begins to vibrate, in preparation for another intervention by Panna. 'Technique can only produce a technical approach. That amounts to nothing more than producing a mechanical brain. The human mind is not a mechanical device: can we not say that this way of regarding the human brain as a mechanical device is at the root of the whole problem? Current

'Surely, technique is secondary; and if technique is the only thing we are striving for, we are obviously denying what is by far the greater part of life. Life is pain, joy, beauty, ugliness, love, and when we understand it as a whole, at every level, that understanding creates its own technique. But the contrary is not true: technique can never bring about creative understanding'.

– *Friend on the Bench*[1]

education has only produced mechanical devices. In fact in today's digital era the kind of children we have come to deal with appear to be like skimming machines. I am shocked to learn that there are institutions that offer courses about what PhDs will need to know to be successful faculty members. These courses deal with career stages that need to be successfully navigated to get a job, surviving as an assistant professor, getting tenure and other professional roles such as being a journal editor, consultant, or department chair.'

There is a pause. I decide to intervene. 'So what do you think we should do with business schools, GP? They have become an integral part of careers in the business world. Do you want them to shut down?'

GP smiles. 'This is not going to happen any case. Do you know that Martin Parker, management professor at Bristol University's Department of Management, wrote a book titled *Shut Down the Business Schools: What's Wrong with Management Education?* In this he laments the lack of a humanistic approach to business education and how business schools have become champions of market economy. These management institutions seem to have become breeding grounds of 'managerial capitalism'.'

'Or breeding grounds of visionary delusions,' I muse.

'Yes, they are very much part of today's creation of unicorns and entrepreneurs chasing their dreams of becoming members of 'three coma clubs'.'

'Three commas?'

'That is shorthand for having a billion dollars of wealth, HC.'

'Ah, I see.'

'These business schools get huge donations from their wealthy alumni. I understand Harvard and Stanford Business Schools have enormous endowments to the value of scores of $billions under their management.'

'Could you say, GP, that with endowments on this scale, the description of them as business schools is misleading? In reality they are fund managers. It appears the management education they offer is incidental.'

'And that is not all. Some business schools talk of offering courses on happiness and even money back guarantees if happiness is not attained. On one level all this sounds ridiculous. Then, more seriously, consider the fate of the young minds who take these courses. Could we call it a simple case of exchanging ignorance?'

'Or maybe we need to devise a new title for these schools: Global Exchange of Delusions, another category of Stock Exchanges?'

Once again the Bluetooth speaker vibrates. 'We cannot be so foolish as to say 'shut down' the Business Schools by bringing in bulldozers as Martin Parker says in his book,' Panna begins. 'They are huge institutions with great properties like land and buildings, not to speak of the money at their disposal. We come back to our core approach, which is to examine the whole of life first and then the details. Grasping the whole of life is about being aware. We are talking of awareness per se, that is the totality of awareness, not just being aware of the climate crisis or war somewhere in the world or being aware of this or that particular issue. We are speaking about being aware of the inner responses also in relation to the outer issues. The business schools should start by bringing this awareness to the students. Students need to understand that life is the whole and the job they do is only a part of life, and not the other way round. Then they have to understand the whole world of jobs before evaluating their particular job. We have to leave it to the wisdom of the management of these business schools to decide whether to be honest and say that the core of management cannot be taught; then, secondly, let the student know the value of business education and all the knowledge that goes with it; and thirdly enable the students to realize the limits of this knowledge. Students need to be aware of all this.'

'Can a human being tell another, educate another to grow in beauty, grow in goodness, flower in great affection and care? If we don't do that, we are destroying the earth, as is happening now, polluting the air. We are destroying everything we touch. So this becomes a very, very serious thing when we talk about beauty, when we talk about pleasure, fear, relationship, order and so on, all that. None of these things are being taught in schools.'

*- Friend on the Bench*[2]

GP looks thoughtful. 'Steve Jobs and Bill Gates are undoubtedly two of the most successful businessmen the world has known. But they did not attend any business school. Harold Geneen as CEO of ITT was generally critical of business schools. In fact he felt that the emphasis is lopsided in business schools. According to him too much attention is paid to the mechanics and not enough to the emotional values of good business management. The greatest problem with management schools is they don't talk of awareness and the significance of awareness in one's life at all. Their focus is essentially on effects. Perhaps today's business education is about 'reconciliation of effects'—which is what politics is about also.'

'According to my understanding,' responds Panna, 'the crisis in the world is the crisis in consciousness of human beings. If this is difficult to follow, business schools should at least understand there are always causes and effects, and effects becoming further causes. This is an endless chain of cause-effect-cause. Without understanding the deeper causes of problems at hand, providing symptomatic solutions will lead nowhere.'

'Yes, and this is worth considering for business schools, if they want to keep claiming that their mission is to make the world a better place. Otherwise they are letting the phenomenon of blindness prevail in the world—where a blind person leads another blind person. Using electric vehicles is a good way of combatting climate degradation. But simply telling people to use electric vehicles is a form of preaching which relies on the force of authority. One needs to have a right relationship to nature and one's own means of transport. Without this understanding, it is only reconciliation of effects that one is resorting to, without ever getting to the causes. Relying on reconciliation of effects is like expecting a neem tree to yield apples.'

'What exactly do you mean by a blind person, Panna?' I ask.

'As long as one lets one's background conditioning interfere with what one is listening to or seeing, and one is not aware of this interference, it is only a fragmented function. What do you call a person who is resorting to this fragmented seeing or listening? If you don't like to say this person is blind, then it may be termed a modified blindness. Seeing becomes 'modified blindness' and listening becomes 'modified deafness'.

'Instead of developing an integrated student who needs to have at least an intellectual understanding that the job they do is an integral part of life and not separate from it, the business schools start from the assumption that work and life are quite separate. Unfortunately, these business schools don't even begin to foster the awareness we have been speaking of. For them awareness could mean being aware of the problems of social conditions and not the inner condition of the mind. The metaphor of two horses drawing the cart illustrates this. One horse, the academic side, is given all the importance whereas the other horse, understanding of life, is so undeveloped that this side has become lame. As a result the cart keeps moving in a lopsided manner. Unfortunately, business schools completely ignore the fact that understanding the operations of the mind is the key to resolving the problems individuals face in life itself. They need to understand that the job their students take up later on is a part of life and not a separate matter to be dealt with apart from life.'

GP looks pensive. Then he offers this: 'One useful purpose the business schools certainly serve today is helping the student get recruited on campus, when big companies go for campus recruitment. Essentially business schools are about networking and contacts. Nitin Nohria, who served as Dean of Harvard Business School for over a decade, wrote in an article in Harvard Business Review in December 2021 about what stood out for the students during their study at Harvard Business School. He based the article on interviews with students: the majority said that the most important value they gained from their time in their MBA program was about contacts and friendships. These contacts certainly have a value, as they also can win for their businesses some reference deals with their connections; this is an especially good thing for start-up companies. In terms of 'making the world a better place', the management of these schools might start by becoming aware of the kind of education they are in fact offering. They certainly need to stop talking about happiness courses. Offering courses on climate control, ethics and values in business seems to be more a matter of fashion. Martin Parker points out that business schools are often used as shorthand for 'some combination of greed and stupidity. Existential threats such as climate change amount to nothing more than modules on 'business ethics'.' It is important to note that in this context ethics and morality are merely effects. They seem to be tacked on as extras rather than emerging as natural products of the ground of order within.'

There is a slight crackle from the Bluetooth speaker. 'Business education does not seem to realize that the description is not the described,' responds Panna. 'Unfortunately, business schools are more about descriptions.'

'And if the business schools have real concern for the welfare of the society,' continues GP, 'they need to understand Peter Drucker's insight that management is not just business management but has become the major regulating mechanism of society. Take the simple case of flying. The price of the flight tickets varies according to when you book. In general the earlier you buy, the cheaper they are. Closer to the departure time prices shoot up.'

'Though sometimes, rather mysteriously, the price goes down again very close to the departure time—presumably because they have failed to sell tickets at the extortionate price,' I put in.

'In this case you may be smarter than me, HC! But this kind of pricing is taught in management schools under the title 'yield management'. One may be aware of the 'surge pricing' adopted by taxi companies like Uber. This 'surge pricing' is also part of 'yield management'. There is an extra price to pay, on an aeroplane, for sitting in a seat which has moderately comfortable legroom, rather than one where you are squeezed in like a cow in a cattle pen. This is another case of 'yield management', which amounts to nothing more than exploiting the needy and desperate. Airlines have cut corners when it comes to hospitality. Most of them have stopped serving food as part of their inflight services unless it is a long-haul flight. They charge you for whatever food they serve as according to the regulations for short haul flights they are not obliged to serve anything other than water. Gone are the days when airlines used to compete by offering better quality of food. All these cost cutting measures have evolved alongside the evolution of management. How far business education is the cause of these trends is a moot point.'

'So,' I offer, 'can we prescribe a 'model' to foster awareness in students—and indeed the faculty? 'Models' after all are what any professor of management or business education wants.'

There is another crackle from the Bluetooth speaker. 'Let us examine this together. First of all we have to examine the state of mind which is raising these questions. For every question we need an answer and most of the time we think the answer lies somewhere outside. This is part of the conditioning of the mind. Asking for models to understand life itself is part of the conditioning. Secondly, we are talking of human spontaneity. Can this be cultivated by any technique or model? Modelling is a term used in engineering and also in financing businesses. In Finance Management also one uses this term very frequently. 'What is the business model' is a standard question of any venture capitalist and investor when evaluating investment in a tech start-up venture.

## To sit under a tree

'You see, you are not educated to be alone. Do you ever go out for a walk by yourself? It is very important to go out alone, to sit under a tree—not with a book, not with a companion, but by yourself—and observe the falling of a leaf, hear the lapping of the water, the fishermen's song, watch the flight of a bird, and of your own thoughts as they chase each other across the space of your mind. If you are able to be alone and watch these things, then you will discover extraordinary riches which no government can tax, no human agency can corrupt, and which can never be destroyed.'

*– Friend on the Bench*[3]

Speaking in terms of models may have validity in a functional domain. But can there be a model to understand life as a whole? Can we bring about human spontaneity by following any model? How can that be called spontaneity if we have a mechanical process? Academics are often conditioned to think that for every problem they encounter they need a solution—a quick solution which many times is a quick fix. In the psychological domain as we have said before things work differently. In the psychological domain there is no place for 'how'. There can be 'knowhow' for a function or in the physical domain, but there is no 'how' concerning understanding the psychological structure of the human mind. The demand for a method or a model-based management course here is nonsensical. No method can tell you how to be aware of things. Because once you practise something, the mind gets caught in practice. As a result, attention gets diluted, and the mind becomes incapable of deep search. Practice could imply learning a few tricks. While driving a vehicle, you simply pay attention to the driving. There are no tricks to this.

'This understanding of life is a natural process. Business schools need to appreciate that not every type of learning is based on assignments and case studies. If business schools were to encourage this, they also would need to have non-assignment based or non-case study approach in addition to what they are doing.

'Most importantly business schools don't educate the students about basic aspects of life such as relationship, knowledge and time. Conventionally speaking relationship implies what exists between a boy and a girl. But relationship exists with everything, including ideas and property around you, as we have already discussed. There is a relationship one has with one's job, one's academic background,

## Thought—how it works.

'Thought is important in its right place, but it has no importance whatsoever psychologically. Thought is the reaction of memory, it is born from memory. Memory is experience as knowledge stored up in the brain cells. You can watch your own brain, you don't have to become a specialist. The brain cells hold memory; it is a material process.'

*– Friend on the Bench*[4]

one's car and so on. It exists with something or another all the time and so is a live thing as it keeps moving from one thing to another.'

GP chuckles. 'If you utter the word 'time' in any business school I expect the minds of professors and students will immediately jump to 'time management' or 'time and motion studies'.'

'What do you say about time, my dear Panna?' I ask.

'I can only share my understanding here as it was explained to me. I cannot pose as an authority. Time exists chronologically. If I want to fly from London to Zurich you can say it takes one and half hours. But psychologically does time exist? I understand the concept of time does not exist psychologically. There is only now. There is no psychological future. One has to feel this deeply to understand this.'

'I'm not sure I understand. Can you explain further, Panna?'

'Perhaps you may be aware that the sense of inadequacy you have experienced in your psyche since childhood—and this goes for all of us—continues even now. Has it undergone any change over time? You think you will be a better human being after some time—say, a few months. So, you depend on time to become a better human being. In that case don't you think that you are depending on a non-existent factor? You see no change in your mental state. Always you have that sense of inadequacy. If you want to change you need to change "now".'

'Very true.'

'Similarly, knowledge has to be understood in its depth, that is its origin, structure, implications. What needs to be understood is 'knowledge' itself instead of getting into a race of acquiring knowledge of this or that. We are talking of knowledge as knowledge itself. Knowledge includes experience. All your experience is also part of knowledge stored in the brain as memory. If you observe carefully, you can understand that thought is nothing but the response of memory. This is a mechanical process: it works in the same way as a search engine such as Google—where you put in a search word

'The answer is in the problem, not away from the problem.'

– *Friend on the Bench*[5]

'We are pointing out that the self is nothing but words and memories.'

– *Friend on the Bench*[6]

and Google immediately searches in its 'memory' and provides the answer. Similarly, the brain produces the response by checking the records available in its memory or sometimes it processes these bits of past information and produces the response. This processing is part of the conditioning. This is a pure material process where there is an input and output produced by the processing. Our thought is no different. It is all the time fetching responses from the stored memory. As long as we think within the confines of the stored memory we are like machines and our lives are nothing but mechanical. What we are trying to point out here is that there is something beyond thought which human beings are capable of. That is what is referred to as intelligence or awareness. This is at a different level than that of thought. In other words, it is like the difference between reading the lines and reading in between the lines. This difference is not something that can be called 'mechanical'.'

'I think I understand, but please carry on.'

'First of all knowledge and experience are required in carrying out any function. If you want to reach your home from the office you need to have the knowledge of the route. But it has no place psychologically. You can't think you are superior to someone who has less knowledge. This idea of superiority or inferiority is a psychological construct. The relationship one has with knowledge is for a functional purpose. When this relationship spills into the psychological domain from a physical domain the disorder begins. You may test this out in your own way.

'There is another dimension of knowledge or truth about knowledge if you will. Knowledge is always incomplete. There is no complete knowledge about anything.'

'Say more.'

'Knowledge is always growing unless it is about a dead matter. New knowledge is being added to old knowledge all the time; anything that can be added to is incomplete. In that sense, you may check out if knowledge is complete or incomplete. This is another

## Making the world a better place

'To help another, you must know yourself, like you, he is the result of the past. We are all interrelated. If you are inwardly diseased by ignorance and ill will, you will inevitably spread disease and darkness. If you are inwardly healthy and integrated, you spread light and peace; otherwise you help to produce greater chaos, greater misery.'

*– Friend on the Bench*[7]

'You cannot train yourself to be attentive. But you can be aware that you are inattentive. And when you are aware that you are inattentive, you are attentive.'

– *Friend on the Bench*[8]

side to knowledge one should bear in mind. Knowledge always travels in the shadow of ignorance.'

'So, Panna, are you saying business schools should educate the students about awareness, relationship, knowledge, time?'

'You are asking me? Who am I to instruct anybody? It is left to the wisdom of the management of these business schools what they want to do. One can see the contradictions in their approach and the fragmented approach in their way of educating students.'

'And if you have actually had an opportunity to do something in this matter, what would you do?'

'What I do is no different from what I have said here. First of all exposure to what my Friend on the Bench said about all these matters and life in general has had, for me, and perhaps for you too, the greatest value in life. That could at least bring in the value of awareness in life and make the students aware that they need to understand profound matters such as time, knowledge, relationship, the nature of thought, the art of living which includes the art of listening, the art of seeing, the art of questioning, the art of learning and so on. None of these things is commercial and there is no way anybody can set up a shop to dispense these. So one has to understand these directly from the source.'

'And how do you respond to what many gurus in the world try to offer in the name of happiness, peace and so on?'

'Oh, I get it. When anybody tries to sell these things their minds are already in the marketplace. What the Friend on the Bench has offered and made others aware of are inward riches, which no guru can give and nobody can rob or tax. Business schools talk of making the world a better place, I don't know how they can achieve this with the current education they provide.

'I would like business schools to expose their students to these vital aspects of life. It is up to the individual student concerned to take this seriously or not. The best that business schools can do is bring in awareness of the existence of these basic things, that is 'awareness per se' and not just awareness of this or that.

'Then, the issue of the sense of inadequacy exists in most of us human beings. Here is not the place to go into this subject in greater depth, as the Friend on the Bench has done, to discuss how we become aware of the sense of inadequacy, to discuss how time, knowledge and relationships are to be understood. These have been among the main concerns of the Friend on the Bench throughout his life. He went around the world talking to hundreds of thousands of people about these things in a thousand different ways for over sixty years.

'As we have said awareness cannot be taught by anybody: one has to be alert and understand this truth oneself. One thought that can be offered to business schools is that they encourage their students to write down their own thoughts and feelings at the end of the day. This would be purely for the benefit of the individual and not a graded assignment. Students would not need to show these notes to their professor and might tear them up after writing them down. It is not like homework. It is part of their own self-discovery.

'The idea is to write down what takes place under the skin as it were and not what you ate for breakfast, what time you left your dorm, how much time it took to reach the class room from the dorm and other mundane details. And there is no aim of making this writing a new method or a new technique. Once a mind gets caught in a technique it soon turns into a mechanical process. Since the whole purpose of this exercise is to develop the human side of the mind, any technique can become a hurdle in the process. Not just a hurdle: it can further strengthen the mechanical part of the brain. The student has to check this out for herself and see if this can enable a self-discovery. What is important is not the determination or the motive of the student but what she discovers. I think this can be good beginning in the process of self-discovery.

'Do not treat this writing down as a new method, a new technique. Try it. But what is important is to become aware of every thought-feeling, from which arises self-knowledge. You must start out on the journey of self-discovery; what you find does not depend on any technique—technique prevents discovery—and it is the discovery that is liberating and creative. What is important is not your determination, conclusion, choice, but what you discover, for that will bring understanding.' 'But, if you have a motive,—that by writing down your thoughts you will put an end to thinking,—then obviously the thing becomes a diary. Because you want a result; and it's very easy to produce a result. You can have an end and achieve a goal—but that does not mean you understand the whole process of yourself, the total process of yourself. The intention is, surely, not how to achieve a result, but to understand yourself, and also to understand why the mind craves for a result. In achieving a result the mind feels secure, there is a satisfaction, a sense of permanency, a vanity, a conceit.'

*– Friend on the Bench*[9]

'The second thing the schools can do is to encourage the students to go out for a walk alone or to sit under a tree, not in the company of their girlfriend or boyfriend. Certainly not carrying a book to read or a mobile phone to check constantly. We already mentioned this in our discussion of work-life balance where we talked of coffee darshan.

'Let the students try this and see what happens. Certainly it causes no harm and the students have nothing to lose.'

# 19

# The Friend on the Bench
## *Awakening of intelligence*

The time has come to say a little more about the man we have called the Friend on the Bench.

There was once a doctor, a very famous person whose reputation had spread far and wide. He was able to cure people of difficult diseases and was known to have very good diagnostic powers. He was being congratulated at a special ceremony in a large town by people who had benefited from his diagnosis and treatment. At this ceremony, he was asked to say a few words:

'I know that all of you think of me as a good doctor, someone who is good at diagnosis and cure,' he began. 'While I'm happy to be amongst you and grateful that you have benefited from my work, I have to say honestly that there are many doctors who are vastly superior to me, who are relatively unknown. The best doctor I know is not known to you at all.

'I have an elder brother who lives in a faraway village and his name is familiar to all the people in that village. He is an excellent doctor who makes sure that whatever disease comes to the village doesn't go out of the village. His name is well known in the village but nobody elsewhere knows his name. He stops disease from spreading and contains it within the village where he lives. He is an eminent doctor and far better than me at diagnosis but his name, as I say, has not gone beyond his village.

'I have another brother who is even less known. He sees disease approaching the village; he can smell it and feel it. And he takes precautions to see that nobody in the village is affected by the disease. Therefore nobody knows his name even in his village.

'You can now decide who is a better doctor. One who smells disease and make sure that nobody falls ill, or one who makes sure that disease does not spread once it has manifested itself, or one who treats disease after it has spread and after all the symptoms are visible. I belong to the last category and my two elder brothers belong to the other two realms.'

We could say the Friend on the Bench is like the eldest brother. He talked of living without problems. His observation is that the way we live creates its own problem and we live trying to solve the problems. When someone asked him what one has to do in life he said 'live simply, stripped of all stupidities, in that beautiful and ecstatic sense.'

When a person dreams that she is dying of thirst in a desert, the glass of water on the bedside is of no use. But someone comes and wakes her up to tell that it is all a dream and a water bottle is there on the bedside. The Friend on the Bench is that someone who wakes one up without claiming any credit. When someone pointed out that the Friend on the Bench had shown him so much, he responded that he has shown nothing: it is all there. He does of course point things out but it is up to the person concerned to see it or not see it.

'Life may not have security, life is meant to be lived.'

– *Friend on the Bench*[1]

'I think one should be able to look at the world, not only nature, the tree, the birds, the flowers and the beauty of life outside, but also look into oneself clearly, because there is all the history of mankind—the struggles, ambitions, drives, temptations, arrogance, violence, stupidity—everything is there. So shouldn't you be concerned with all this, not just fragments of life? If one is so concerned, out of that comes intelligence. Out of intelligence, one acts.'

*– Friend on the Bench*[2]

The Friend on the Bench's real name was Jiddu Krishnamurti. As a young man in southern India he was chosen to be the world teacher by the luminaries of the Theosophical Society. But after a few years he renounced this position and all that went with it, saying his only concern was to set man free totally and unconditionally. He dissolved the Order specifically set up by the Theosophists, which by the 1920s has some 40,000 international members, and gave back 5000 acres of land in Holland to the original donor. He declared to those who considered themselves his followers that 'Truth is a pathless land'. Henceforth he would travel the world giving talks and engaging people in conversation and questioning—not in the manner of an expert who knows the truth but in the manner of a friend sitting on a bench in a park, someone to whom you expose your feelings, thoughts, ideas. Sometimes the process could be uncomfortable or even disturbing but such disturbance he said could hold the key to understand the truth of life—so long as the dialogue is caried out with deep affection and respect.

Some have called him a philosopher but he was not a philosopher in the sense of someone expounding a theory. His concern was the human condition, suffering, fear, pleasure, pain. The logic of software known as 'if this then that' or ITTT pervaded his whole exposition of life, thus bringing an objective outlook to subjective matters. As his friend the physicist David Bohm made clear, the Friend on the Bench had no theory or system to expound. There is no set of techniques to discover here.

The Friend on the Bench does not consider himself an authority. 'He has made certain discoveries,' wrote Bohm, 'and he is simply doing his best to make those discoveries accessible to all those who are prepared to listen. He is certainly not aiming to set up any new system of religious belief. Rather it is up to each human being to see if he can discover for himself that to which K is calling attention, and to go on from there to make new discoveries on his own.'

All his mature life the Friend on the Bench was deeply concerned with the question of education—partly out of dissatisfaction with the prevalent modes of education which he considered damaging, even deadening. Education for him was not a matter of inculcating knowledge through discipline—the method that is in vogue throughout the world—but rather of awakening and keeping alive the flame of compassionate intelligence, the natural curiosity and wonderment which he saw present in all young children. To this end he founded schools, in India, in the UK and in California.

Exploration, inquiry, and questioning were requisite states of mind when discussing with Krishnamurti, either privately in an interview or publicly in a question-and-answer sessions. He encouraged his listeners to experiment with the teachings, to find out for themselves if what he said was true or not and then challenge him: 'Tear it to pieces,' he counselled: 'see if it is the truth.'

Why is the Friend on the Bench present in this book? Both GP and I encountered his talks and dialogues, at different times and in different places, at some point in mid-life when we were both beginning to ponder the questions of living in more depth. Neither of us was seeking a guru, someone who would answer these questions for us. Rather we were looking for someone who would help us pose these questions more deeply and perhaps more uncomfortably. All his mature life the Friend on the Bench was clear that he was not a guru—even though inevitably some looked up to him as such. Rather than accumulating personal wealth and honors he consistently renounced them. When he was awarded the prestigious Templeton Prize in 1984, he didn't take it, saying the work he did should not be paid.

'I want to be your companion with the freshness of the breeze.'

*– Friend on the Bench*[3]

'First of all there is no speaker, as we pointed out the other day. You are speaking to yourself, you are looking at yourself. The speaker may be the mirror, but the mirror has no value. You use the telephone to speak, but the telephone itself has very little importance. What you say in the telephone is important. So similarly, there is no speaker here.'

*– Friend on the Bench*[4]

# Epilogue

## *Water in the hill*

---

It's our last morning at the School in the Valley, and after breakfast and a short walk around the campus and the bird sanctuary, time for goodbyes. I'm sorry to be leaving: this place in the magnificent landscape of red weathered rocks has a special magic. The spirit of the Friend on the Bench, who was last here nearly forty years ago, remains as something like a fresh and subtle breeze. Our time here has been relaxing, rich in conversations with friends and experiences of beauty, and also productive for the progress of our book.

We are heading back to the city of minarets, GP's home city, but he has mentioned that we are making a small detour. Wet Hill, the village where we started this book, is not far away, just to the east of the main highway. This time we are heading north, so the sun seems to burn a little less brightly, and the hills are on our left-hand side. There's something there GP wants to show me, a water project.

'So tell me about this water project, GP. What exactly are we going to see?'

'This is something I am helping with, HC, but it was not my idea originally. This is a scheme conjured by farmers of the village, Wet Hill, and neighbouring villages. It all comes from the fact that the river to the north of the village dried up quite a while ago, and that meant there was no possibility of irrigation for the wet crops.'

'Quite a serious matter for the villages, I imagine.'

'Oh yes, it reduced their income very considerably. Some could hardly survive. But then one or two of them thought about the range of hills to the south of the village, much more extensive than the range to the north, some 20km in depth from north to south. Here, they realized, there were possibilities to build a dam and store rain water, and then pass it down through water channels to the villages. And then a group of the farmers approached me: I looked at the scheme, consulted with an agronomist friend and decided to help.'

'So what does it actually consist of?'

'There's a check dam with a retaining wall 15 metres high and 10 km of channels. This gives the possibility of irrigating thousands of hectares of wet crops.'

'What an ingenious idea they had and how good you could help.'

Suddenly the figure on the dashboard begins to vibrate: 'the hills to the south are retaining moisture,' comments Panna, 'so it is now truly a Wet Hill.'

We are close to Wet Hill now, and at a junction just outside the village, as apparently prearranged by GP, we are joined by a childhood friend of his. He directs us for a few kilometres to a nearby village. He wants to show us a particular house, which doesn't stand out from the other dwellings in this very ordinary place. This was the birthplace of a man who became a prominent politician and eventually President of the country.

We are back in the car, heading for Wet Hill, and the figure on the dashboard vibrates once more. 'The remarkable thing here is not the outward appearance, as you saw. What was remarkable was the state of mind of this man, the politician who became President of the country. That is the real ground of life itself. The outer things are there but the perspective of life comes from within.'

When we reach Wet Hill we are met by a small delegation of villagers. From the way they greet GP I can see the affection and respect they hold for him, and vice versa. We leave our car in the village square—the place where the bus arrives and departs, and close to the bench, of sturdy construction, dating back to the days of the British raj, where once a distinguished-looking man, dressed in traditional garb, used to engage in discussion with village elders on the state of the world.

We transfer to two larger SUV-type vehicles, which can manage the steep climb up through the hills to the check dam. We get out; it's quiet and peaceful here, with no human habitation in sight, and just the birds of prey circling high overhead. We clamber over rocks to the edge of the retaining wall, which is now almost complete. I can imagine the reservoir that will soon resemble a lake, sending water through the channels to irrigate the crops in the fields below the hills.

GP and I are back in the car, heading for the city of minarets. This time the journey is an untroubled one: we don't encounter any roadblocks.

After an hour or so I break the silence: 'I feel that what we have talked about during this trip was not just relevant to management, GP. Some of it touched on matters you could call spiritual, or religious.'

The figure on the dashboard vibrates, for one last time. 'We need to be very careful in the usage of words,' insists Panna. His voice seems to have acquired an even deeper resonance. 'First of all I am not sure we know what is meant by these words, spiritual or religious. What is important is to lead a life that is inclined towards order inside and order outside, not to create disorder to anyone or anything one deals with and as far as possible not waste energy on frivolous pursuits that may lead us astray. This is the truth of the matter and not giving high-sounding names to things—names which may not have much meaning.

'Management which is called administration in the context of a school or a non-profit or whatever job one does, is not separate from life but it is part of life. I hope your book will not be one of those about going to seek wisdom from some sage in the East. This is a meaningless assumption. As you have already discussed, there are many executives from the West who find their way to India or the Himalayas to 'seek wisdom', but in fact their purpose is to set up a successful venture to make millions or billions of dollars.

'It means we have reduced the significance of wisdom to a petty little purpose. I think to understand the operations of one's own mind is at the core of wisdom and it is possible to go through this process wherever one lives, in the course of ordinary daily life. One does not need to go to a special place, an ashram in the Himalayas, to find wisdom.'

Panna's voice continues to resonate after he has finished speaking. Eventually I break the silence one more time. 'What we tried to say is that one has to start near to go far. Near is one's state of mind. That is where we need to start, and then we can travel, maybe as far as we want or need to go.'

GP says nothing but touches a button on the car's music system. His choice again is Neil Young's 'Heart of Gold' –

'I want to live, I want to give

I have been a miner searching for a heart of gold---'

# Notes

All the books listed here are of J. Krishnamurti and published by the Krishnamurti Foundations located in India, England and the United States of America.

**1. The Why of the Book: *In the spirit of bus-pushers***
1. *Collected Works*, Vol. 15, 2024.

**6. Understanding Operations of the Mind: *Core of management***
1. *Magnitude of the Mind*, 2000.
2. *The Revolution from Within*, 1999.
3. *The Revolution from Within*, 1999.
4. *What Are You Doing with Your Life?* 2002.
5. *What Are You Doing with Your Life?* 2002.
6. *Collected Works*, Vol. 3, 2024.
7. *Collected Works*, Vol. 3, 2024.
8. *The Revolution from Within*, 1999.

**7. Result of Time: *Time and conditioning***
1. Saanen, 1978, Public Talk 2.
2. *Collected Works*, Vol. 3, 2024.

**10. Work-Life Balance: *Coffee darshan, a pause in the day***
1. *The Book of Life*, 2021.
2. *Collected Works*, Vol. 4, 2024.

3. *Saanen*, 1978, Public Talk 2.
4. *How to Find Peace (Social Responsibility)*, 2007.
5. *How to Find Peace (Social Responsibility)*, 2007.
6. *The Mirror of Relationship*, 2001.
7. *On Relationship*, 1999.
8. *Leaving School, Entering Life*, 2018.
9. *Leaving School, Entering Life*, 2018.

**12. Role Models:** *And second-hand human beings*
1. *A Wholly Different Way of Living*, 2000.
2. *Mis diálogos con Jiddu Krishnamurti*, by Feldman Gonzalez Rubén, Orion Editorial, 2013.

**13. Investors:** *Illusions, damned illusions and investor's dreams*
1. *Collected Works*, Vol. 2, 2024

**17. Productivity:** *Three immutable laws*
1. *This Light in Oneself*, 2002.
2. *The First and Last Freedom*, 2001.
3. *The Book of Life*, 2021.

**18. Beyond Business Schools:** *Nurturing the second horse*
1. *Education and Significance of Life*, 1992.
2. *A Wholly Different Way of Living*, 2000.
3. *Think on These Things*, 2007.
4. *This Light In Oneself*, 2002.
5. *Collected Works*, Vol. 7, 2024.
6. *On Mind and Thought*, 2004.
7. *What Are You Looking for?* 2022.
8. *Collected Works*, Vol.16, 2024.
9. *Collected Works*, Vol. 3, 2024

**19. The Friend on the Bench:** *Awakening of Intelligence*
1. *The Last Talks*, 2024.
2. *Brockwood Park*, 1969, Discussion with Students and Staff, 1970.
3. *Life in Freedom (Early Works)*, 1928.
4. *Saanen*, 1978, Public Talk 2.

# About the Author

Vishwanath Alluri, whose academic background is in chartered accountancy and company secretaryship, worked as a finance manager and later went on to have a three-decades-long career as a CEO. Though not an engineer, he became a tech entrepreneur and has founded IMImobile, which specialized in mobile data infrastructure, and having developed cPaaS (communication Platform as a Service). IMImobile had equity investors from India, the UK and the USA. Vish had many international laurels to his name. IMImobile, having been listed on the London Stock Exchange's AIM, was acquired by CISCO in 2021. Prior to this, his engineering software unit was acquired by a Danish Engineering Conglomerate. Vish has also produced two films.

# About the Co-author

Harry Eyres is a writer, journalist and poet, best known for the column 'Slow Lane' in the *Financial Times* weekend edition, which he created and wrote weekly from 2004 to 2015. He has also been a theatre critic and arts writer for *The Times*, poetry editor of *The Daily Express* and wine columnist for several leading publications. He is the author of the memoir *Horace and Me: Life Lessons from an Ancient Poet* (Bloomsbury and Farrar, Straus & Giroux), shortlisted for the PEN Ackerley Prize, two collections of poetry and several books on wine.

# HarperCollins *Publishers* India

At HarperCollins India, we believe in telling the best stories and finding the widest readership for our books in every format possible. We started publishing in 1992; a great deal has changed since then, but what has remained constant is the passion with which our authors write their books, the love with which readers receive them, and the sheer joy and excitement that we as publishers feel in being a part of the publishing process.

Over the years, we've had the pleasure of publishing some of the finest writing from the subcontinent and around the world, including several award-winning titles and some of the biggest bestsellers in India's publishing history. But nothing has meant more to us than the fact that millions of people have read the books we published, and that somewhere, a book of ours might have made a difference.

As we look to the future, we go back to that one word— a word which has been a driving force for us all these years.

Read.